IDs—Not That Easy

Questions About Nationwide Identity Systems

Stephen T. Kent and Lynette I. Millett, *Editors*

Committee on Authentication Technologies and
Their Privacy Implications

Computer Science and Telecommunications Board

Division on Engineering and Physical Sciences

National Research Council

NATIONAL ACADEMY PRESS
Washington, D.C.

NATIONAL ACADEMY PRESS • 2101 Constitution Avenue, N.W. • Washington DC 20418

NOTICE: The project from which this report was generated was approved by the Governing Board of the National Research Council, whose members are drawn from the councils of the National Academy of Sciences, the National Academy of Engineering, and the Institute of Medicine. The members of the committee responsible for the report were chosen for their special competences and with regard for appropriate balance.

Support for this project was provided by the National Science Foundation, the Office of Naval Research, the General Services Administration, the Federal Chief Information Officers' Council, and the Social Security Administration. Support for this special report was provided by the Vadasz Family Foundation, a contributor to the Computer Science and Telecommunications Board's program on information technology and society. Any opinions, findings, conclusions, or recommendations expressed in this material are those of the authors and do not necessarily reflect the views of the sponsors.

International Standard Book Number 0-309-08430-X

Additional copies of this report are available from:

National Academy Press
2101 Constitution Avenue, N.W.
Box 285
Washington, DC 20055
800/624-6242
202/334-3313 (in the Washington metropolitan area)

The report is also available online at <http://www.nap.edu> and <http://www.cstb.org/>

THE NATIONAL ACADEMIES

National Academy of Sciences
National Academy of Engineering
Institute of Medicine
National Research Council

The **National Academy of Sciences** is a private, nonprofit, self-perpetuating society of distinguished scholars engaged in scientific and engineering research, dedicated to the furtherance of science and technology and to their use for the general welfare. Upon the authority of the charter granted to it by the Congress in 1863, the Academy has a mandate that requires it to advise the federal government on scientific and technical matters. Dr. Bruce M. Alberts is president of the National Academy of Sciences.

The **National Academy of Engineering** was established in 1964, under the charter of the National Academy of Sciences, as a parallel organization of outstanding engineers. It is autonomous in its administration and in the selection of its members, sharing with the National Academy of Sciences the responsibility for advising the federal government. The National Academy of Engineering also sponsors engineering programs aimed at meeting national needs, encourages education and research, and recognizes the superior achievements of engineers. Dr. Wm. A. Wulf is president of the National Academy of Engineering.

The **Institute of Medicine** was established in 1970 by the National Academy of Sciences to secure the services of eminent members of appropriate professions in the examination of policy matters pertaining to the health of the public. The Institute acts under the responsibility given to the National Academy of Sciences by its congressional charter to be an adviser to the federal government and, upon its own initiative, to identify issues of medical care, research, and education. Dr. Kenneth I. Shine is president of the Institute of Medicine.

The **National Research Council** was organized by the National Academy of Sciences in 1916 to associate the broad community of science and technology with the Academy's purposes of furthering knowledge and advising the federal government. Functioning in accordance with general policies determined by the Academy, the Council has become the principal operating agency of both the National Academy of Sciences and the National Academy of Engineering in providing services to the government, the public, and the scientific and engineering communities. The Council is administered jointly by both Academies and the Institute of Medicine. Dr. Bruce M. Alberts and Dr. Wm. A. Wulf are chairman and vice chairman, respectively, of the National Research Council.

Preface

The terrorist attacks of September 11, 2001, and subsequent discussions have brought fresh urgency to the challenges of providing information security. In the wake of these and other recent events, numerous proposals have been circulating both in policy circles and the national media.

One proposal that has received a fair amount of attention is a national identification card—or, more precisely, a nationwide identity system. The Bush administration has indicated that a national identification card is not within the scope of options it is contemplating. Congress, however, has been considering various alternatives—for example, a measure in the Enhanced Border Security and Visa Entry Reform Act of 2001 would require biometric identifiers to be employed on visas and other travel and entry documents for aliens (H.R. 3525, Section 303). Additional suggestions include a proposal by the American Association of Motor Vehicle Administrators (AAMVA) to link state motor vehicle departments and a proposed "trusted traveler" system for airports.

The persistence of public discussion on the topic and the expectation that other proposals will be offered argue for an informed analysis and critique of the concept of a nationwide identity system.

In early 2001, the Computer Science and Telecommunications Board, (CSTB) a unit of the National Research Council with a long history of examining information technology, security, and related issues,[1] launched a study to examine authentication technologies and their privacy implications. Sponsored by the National Science Foundation, the Office of Naval Research, the General Services Administration, the Federal Chief Information Officers' Council, and the Social Security Administration, the study aims to assess emerging approaches to user authentication in computing and communications systems, and it specifically focuses on the implications of these authentication technologies for privacy.

The study is being conducted by the multidisciplinary Committee on Authentication Technologies and Their Privacy Implications, whose members include experts in the design, implementation, deployment, and use of information systems generally and information systems security in particular, along with experts in privacy law and policy (see Appendix A for committee and staff biographies). Given that identification and authentication systems constitute a large portion of the committee's agenda, it is well positioned to comment on the technology and policy issues surrounding a nationwide identity system and its supporting infrastructures (hereinafter referred to as a nationwide identity system). In fact, CSTB asked the committee to do so, in the interest of providing a timely contribution to the public debate. Additional resources from the Vadasz Family Foundation enabled development of this report.

The committee's broader and more comprehensive final report is expected in late 2002, but its members felt compelled to issue a brief report at this time because of the real possibility that further debate on a nationwide identity system, and even action on the topic, could take place prior to the final report's issuance. Thus the present effort outlines the issues the committee believes must be addressed and raises a number of questions that the committee believes should be answered as part of any consideration of a nationwide identity system.

This brief report is a product of the committee's deliberations, drawing on its members' areas of expertise. But, given time and resource limitations, it is not an exhaustive assessment. It is intended to catalyze a

---

[1]See, for example, CSTB reports such as *Growing Vulnerability of the Public Switched Networks* (1989), *Computers at Risk* (1991), *Evolving the High Performance Computing and Communications Initiative to Support the Nation's Information Infrastructure* (1995), *Cryptography's Role in Securing the Information Society* (1996), *For the Record: Protecting Electronic Health Information* (1997), *Trust in Cyberspace* (1999), *The Internet's Coming of Age* (2000), *Embedded, Everywhere: A Research Agenda for Networked Systems of Embedded Computers* (2001), and *Cybersecurity Today and Tomorrow: Pay Now or Pay Later* (2002). See <http://www.cstb.org/web/topic_security> for a complete list of CSTB reports related to security, assurance, and privacy.

broader and more sophisticated discussion. Clearly, the legal, policy, and technological issues associated with nationwide identity systems warrant a much more detailed and comprehensive examination. The committee invites feedback on this brief report as it continues the process of preparing its broader and more in-depth final report on the topic of authentication technologies and their implications for privacy.

The committee thanks David D. Clark, chair of the CSTB, and Marjory S. Blumenthal, CSTB's director, for their commentary and feedback on draft versions of the report. The committee also wishes to thank the various members of the CSTB staff who helped to make it happen. Jennifer Bishop took over as senior project assistant for the authentication study midway through the project, managing logistics, organizing materials, and coping with an unplanned brief report and review with aplomb. She also assisted in developing the diagrams in the report and designed its cover. Janet Briscoe, CSTB's administrative officer, provided crucial administrative and logistical support as well as the suggestion that ultimately led to the report's title. Andy White, director of the NRC's Committee on National Statistics, provided feedback during the formulation and review phases. The committee also thanks Steven J. Marcus, a freelance editor, for assistance at multiple stages of the report's development. Liz Fikre at the National Research Council also made significant editorial contributions to the final manuscript. Lynette Millett is the study director for this project; she synthesized this report, coordinating contributions from committee members and drafting the response to reviewers.

Stephen T. Kent, *Chair*
Committee on Authentication
Technologies and Their
Privacy Implications

Acknowledgment of Reviewers

This report has been reviewed in draft form by individuals chosen for their diverse perspectives and technical expertise, in accordance with procedures approved by the National Research Council's Report Review Committee. The purpose of this independent review is to provide candid and critical comments that will assist the institution in making its published report as sound as possible and to ensure that the report meets institutional standards for objectivity, evidence, and responsiveness to the study charge. The review comments and draft manuscript remain confidential to protect the integrity of the deliberative process. We wish to thank the following individuals for their review of this report:

Alfred Blumstein, Carnegie Mellon University,
Michael Caloyannides, Mitretek Systems, Inc.,
Julie E. Cohen, Georgetown University Law Center,
Jerome H. Saltzer, Massachusetts Institute of Technology,
Peter Swire, George Washington University, and
Lee M. Zeichner, LegalNet Works, Inc.

Although the reviewers listed above have provided many constructive comments and suggestions, they were not asked to endorse the conclusions or recommendations, nor did they see the final draft of the report before its release. The review of this report was overseen by Willis Ware of RAND. Appointed by the National Research Council, he was responsible for making certain that an independent examination of this report was carried out in accordance with institutional procedures and that all review comments were carefully considered. Responsibility for the final content of this report rests entirely with the authoring committee and the institution.

Contents

Executive Summary

Nationwide identity systems have been proposed as a solution for problems ranging from counterterrorism to fraud detection to enabling electoral reforms. In the wake of September 11, 2001, and renewed interest in the topic, the Committee on Authentication Technologies and Their Privacy Implications of the Computer Science and Telecommunications Board[1] developed this short report as part of its ongoing study process, in order to raise questions and catalyze a broader debate about such systems. The committee believes that serious and sustained analysis and discussion of the complex constellation of issues presented by nationwide identity systems are needed. Understanding the goals of such a system is a primary consideration. Indeed, before any decisions can be made about *whether* to attempt some kind of nationwide identity system, the question of *what* is being discussed (and why) must be answered.

There are numerous questions about the desirability and feasibility of a nationwide identity system. This report does not attempt to answer these questions comprehensively and does not propose moving toward such a system or backing away. Instead, it aims to highlight some of the significant and challenging policy, procedural, and technological issues

---

[1]See <http://www.cstb.org/web/project_authentication>.

presented by such a system, with the goal of fostering a broad, deliberate, and sophisticated discussion among policy makers and stakeholders about whether such a system is desirable or feasible.

Policy questions that the committee believes should be considered when contemplating any kind of identity system include the following:

- What is the *purpose of the system*? Possibilities range from expediting and/or tracking travel to prospectively monitoring individuals' activities in order to identify and look for suspicious activity to retrospectively identifying perpetrators of crimes.

- What is the *scope of the population* that would be issued an "ID" and, presumably, be recorded in the system? How would the identities of these individuals be authenticated?

- What is the *scope of the data* that would be gathered about individuals participating in the system and correlated with their national identity? While colloquially it is referred to as an "identification system," implying that all the system would do is identify individuals, many proposals talk about the ID as a key to a much larger collection of data. Would these data be identity data only (and what is meant by identity data)? Or would other data be collected, stored, and/or analyzed as well? With what confidence would the accuracy and quality of this data be established and subsequently determined?

- *Who would be the user(s)* of the system (as opposed to those who would participate in the system by having an ID)? One assumption seems to be that the public sector/government will be the primary user, but what parts of the government, in what contexts, and with what constraints? In what setting(s) in the public sphere would such a system be used? Would state and local governments have access to the system? Would the private sector be allowed to use the system? What entities within the government or private sector would be allowed to use the system? Who could contribute, view, and/or edit data in the system?

- What *types of use* would be allowed? Who would be able to ask for an ID, and under what circumstances? Assuming that there are datasets associated with an individual's identity, what types of queries would be permitted (e.g., "Is this person allowed to travel?" "Does this person have a criminal record?")? Beyond simple queries, would analysis and data mining of the information collected be permitted? If so, who would be allowed to do such analysis and for what purpose(s)?

- Would participation in and/or identification by the system be *voluntary or mandatory*? In addition, would participants have to be aware of or consent to having their IDs checked (as opposed to, for example, allowing surreptitious facial recognition)?

• What *legal structures* protect the system's integrity as well as the data subject's privacy and due process rights, and determine the government and relying parties' liability for system misuse or failure?

Each of these issues is elaborated on in the report. And each of the above questions evokes a larger set of issues and questions that must be resolved. In addition, many of these issues are interdependent, and choices made for each will bear on the options available for resolving other issues.

Decisions made at this level will also have ramifications for the technological underpinnings of the system, including what levels and kinds of system security will be required. In fact, "system" may be the most important (and heretofore least discussed) aspect of the term "nationwide identity system," because it implies the linking together of many social, legal, and technological components in complex and interdependent ways. The success or failure of such a system is dependent not just on the individual components but also on the ways they work—or do not work— together. The control of these interdependencies, and the mitigation of security vulnerabilities and their unintended consequences, would determine the overall effectiveness of the system.

The committee believes that given the complexity and potential impact of nationwide identity systems, more analysis is needed with respect to both desirability and feasibility. In particular,

• Given the potential economic costs, significant design and implementation challenges, and risks to both security and privacy, there should be broad agreement on what problem(s) a nationwide identity system would address. Once there is agreement on the problem(s) to be solved, alternatives to identity systems should also be considered as potential solutions to whatever problem(s) is identified and agreed upon.
• The goals of a nationwide identity system must be clearly and publicly identified and deliberated upon, with input sought from all stakeholders; public review of these goals prior to selecting a proposed system is essential.
• Proponents of such a system should be required to present a very compelling case, addressing the issues raised in this report and soliciting input from a broad range of stakeholder communities.
• Serious consideration must be given to the idea that—given the broad range of uses, security needs, and privacy needs that might be contemplated—no single system may suffice to meet the needs of potential users of the system.

- Care must be taken to explore completely the potential ramifications, because the costs of abandoning, correcting, or redesigning a system after broad deployment might well be extremely high.

The legal, policy, and technological issues associated with nationwide identity systems warrant much more detailed and comprehensive examination and assessment than are presented in this report. The committee hopes that the extensive set of questions and issues raised here will help to both further and inform the policy debate. The committee welcomes feedback on this brief report as it continues preparing its broader and more in-depth final report on the topic of authentication technologies and their privacy implications.

1

Introduction and Overview

W hile the events of September 11, 2001, have galvanized a search for improvements in the safety and security of our society, the challenge is to provide protection without sacrificing fundamental freedoms. An idea that has resurfaced as a result of the attacks is the creation of a "national identity card," often referred to simply as a "national ID."[1] This term is a bit of a misnomer, in that a card would likely be but one component of a large and complex nationwide identity system, the core of which could be a database of personal information on the U.S. population. This report by the Committee on Authentication Technologies and Their Privacy Implications provides a limited exploration of such a system and of the potential legal, policy, and technical challenges that it might present.

No one really knows if a nationwide identity system could detect or deter terrorism, although several arguments have been advanced. One is that such a system could be used to easily identify known terrorists upon their interaction with particular agents (such as airline security officials), facilitating their arrest. On the other hand, unless the database of suspects includes those particular individuals, the best possible identity sys-

---

[1]See, for example, "States Devising Plan for High-Tech National Identification System" at <http://www.washingtonpost.com/wp-dyn/articles/A32717-2001Nov2.html> and "National ID Card Gaining Support" at <http://www.washingtonpost.com/wp-dyn/articles/A52300-2001Dec16.html>.

tem would not lead to their apprehension. Another suggestion is that the data collected from the widespread use of nationwide IDs could help prevent terrorists from achieving their objectives. This might involve the detection of abnormal or suspicious patterns of behavior that accompany the planning and/or execution of a terrorist act.

Another potential role of a nationwide identity system is as an investigative tool in the aftermath of a crime or terrorist attack. Here, the data collected could help retrospectively in the identification, arrest, and prosecution of the perpetrators. Some argue that this is primarily (though not exclusively) a post facto activity, more useful for law enforcement than for counterterrorism, which is, in part, an a priori *intelligence* function.

Terrorism issues per se are beyond the scope of this report, which examines the concept of a nationwide identity system in the large, not solely with respect to counterterrorism. The committee believes that the concept of a nationwide identity system—including *whether* such a system is a good idea—must be examined on its own merits.

Indeed, nationwide identity systems have been sought for many purposes in addition to countering terrorism. They have been proposed to aid in fraud prevention (for example, in the administration of public benefits), catch "deadbeat dads," enable electoral reforms, allow quick background checks for those buying guns or other monitored items, and prevent illegal aliens from working in the United States.

Depending on the nature of the population, the data collected, and the scope of use, a nationwide identity system might be able to help with other tasks as well. For example, a robust, accurate and comprehensive system might aid law-enforcement officials in tracking or finding people.[2] It is possible that the correlation of social (for example, health, economic, demographic) information could be more easily accomplished with the use of a national identity system; statisticians, for example, note how a single identifier would facilitate some of their analyses. In addition, depending on implementation choices, e-commerce and e-government transactions might be simplified. However, there could also be negative consequences, ranging from infringement on rights and liberties (including loss of or invasion of personal privacy) to harm resulting from misidentification or misuse of the system, plus significant implementation and deployment costs. The trade-offs (enhanced security versus risks to pri-

---

[2]Examples include tracking fugitives, executing warrants, tracking noncitizens with expired visas, tracking illegal aliens, and confirming alibis for those innocent of criminal charges. A nationwide identity system could facilitate the work done by the National Crime Information Center, a computerized database at the Federal Bureau of Investigation that permits access by authorized users to documented criminal justice information.

vacy, cost versus functionality, and so on) need to be carefully considered.

Many other countries have nationwide identity systems, which they often use for such diverse purposes as proof of age (e.g., Belgium), proof of citizenship, and for generating electronic signatures (e.g., Finland). In the United States, citizens' concern for civil liberties, their historic association of ID cards with repressive regimes, and states' rights concerns have discouraged movement toward a governmentally sanctioned nationwide identity system.[3] Additionally, because the country was settled by immigrants, a significant fraction of whom wanted to escape just such practices, many U.S. record systems were intentionally designed not to gather linking data.[4] Further, it appears that laws requiring individuals to show proof of legal status or citizenship result in increased discrimination based on national origin and/or appearance.[5] The human rights issues that could arise, such as increased demands for documentation from those who look or sound "foreign" and the deterioration of living and working conditions for aliens, are substantial.[6] Clearly, an examination of the legal and social framework surrounding identity systems, while outside the scope of this report, would be essential.[7]

Although discriminatory acts such as those alluded to above might be constrainable by law, the presentation of identifying documents—driver's licenses and credit cards, for example—is being demanded today in more

---

[3]The Electronic Privacy Information Center has compiled a set of resources and reports on the topic at its Web site, <http://www.epic.org/privacy/id_cards/>.

[4]An example that frustrates many genealogists is that U.S. birth certificates usually require identifying the town of birth only for parents born in the United States; for people born elsewhere, the country of birth is sufficient. Generally speaking, the mindset that such things are "no one's business" has deep roots.

[5]See U.S. General Accounting Office (GAO), *Immigration Reform: Employer Sanctions and the Question of Discrimination*, March 1990; Marvin Howe, "Immigration Law Leads to Job Bias, New York Reports," *New York Times*, February 26, 1990, p. A1. The GAO report on the Immigration Reform and Control Act of 1986 (IRCA) cites a "widespread pattern of discrimination" resulting "solely from the implementation of IRCA." Ten percent of employers discriminated on the basis of foreign accent or appearance, and nine percent discriminated by preferring certain authorized workers over others.

[6]Especially for communities of recent immigrants, there is likely to be significant controversy in shifting to a system that would prohibit or make difficult work and other activities without presentation of an ID. In considering the feasibility and desirability of a particular approach, designers of any such system should be aware of this potential opposition, as well as possible opposition from other segments of the population.

[7]It would be useful to examine how such systems have worked in other countries, as well as to examine nations where IDs have been proposed but not implemented (such as the United Kingdom).

and more generic circumstances. There is also evidence of growing efforts in the public and private sectors to collect, maintain, correlate, and use more and more information on citizens' activities based on existing identifiers such as Social Security numbers (SSNs). Initially designed only for administering social security benefits, SSNs are now common data elements in public and private sector databases, allowing for easy sharing and correlation of disparate records. This is a classic example of function "creep"—continuous expansion in the use of a system first intended for a limited purpose.[8]

Before any decisions can be made about *whether* to attempt to formalize some kind of nationwide identity system, the question of *what* is being discussed must be answered. Thus the committee believes that substantive and sustained analysis is needed on the issue.

There is no recognized universal model for a nationwide identity system. Because different people mean different things when they discuss the concept, evaluating it requires clarification of what is intended. The range of possibilities for identity systems is broad and includes alternative approaches such as the following:

- A database establishing a unique identity and maintaining information on every U.S. citizen, including, for example, information on known felony convictions and place of residence, available for government and commercial query;
- A system similar to the above system that also includes noncitizens who are legally in the United States;[9]

---

[8]Some might argue that the SSN is already a de facto national identifier. The General Accounting Office makes this assertion and also points out that no one law governs the use of SSNs. While originally intended to identify retirees who qualified for the Social Security retirement system, the SSN is now required, in some cases by law, to be used to identify individuals who seek federal assistance. In addition, of course, the SSN has been adopted as a taxpayer ID number. In his book *Database Nation*, Simson Garfinkel provides a history of the expanded use of the SSN. Provisions of the Social Security Act, the Privacy Act, and the Computer Matching Act are among the laws that attempt to limit the conditions under which SSNs and associated data are used (General Accounting Office, *Social Security: Government and Commercial Use of the Social Security Number Is Widespread*, GAO/HEHS-99-28, February 1999). For example, the Privacy Act of 1974, available at <http://www.usdoj.gov/foia/privstat.htm>, requires the disclosure of how the SSN will be used by all government agencies. In 1986, the Office of Technology Assessment addressed the issue of ubiquitous use of the SSN as well (U.S. Congress, Office of Technology Assessment, *Government Information Technology: Electronic Records Systems and Individual Privacy*, OTA-CIT-296, Washington, D.C., U.S. Government Printing Office, June 1986).

[9]Note that there are additional discussions about systems aimed exclusively at noncitizens, including, for example, proposals that would more rigorously track foreign students within the United States.

- A database of only a fraction of the country's population—those individuals who have a specific characteristic (for example, criminal record, past noncriminal but anomalous behavior, trusted travelers)—that would not include the majority of people in the country; and
- A database allowing voluntary participation in return for such benefits as ease of entry into the country or access to the fast line at the airport security checkpoint.

The above possibilities (there are others as well) emphasize the need for answers to a number of questions before a more substantive analysis can proceed. Several policy questions should be asked when considering any kind of identity system (see also Figure 1.1):

- What would be the *purpose of the system*? Possibilities include expediting and/or tracking travel, prospectively monitoring citizens' activities in order to discern suspicious behavior, and retrospectively aiding in the identification of perpetrators of crime, among others.[10]
- What is the *scope of the population* for whom an ID would be issued and whose activities would presumably be recorded in the system? How would the identities of these individuals be authenticated?
- What is the *scope of the data* that would be gathered about individuals participating in the system and correlated with their national identity? While it may be referred to casually as an "identification system," implying that all the system would do is identify individuals, many proposals talk about the ID as a key to a much larger collection of data. Would these data include only identity data (and what, precisely, is meant by identity data)? Or would other data be collected, stored, and/or analyzed as well? With what confidence would the accuracy and quality of these data be established and subsequently determined?
- *Who would be the user(s)* of the system (as opposed to who would participate in the system by having an ID)? One assumption seems to be that the public sector/federal government would be the primary user, but what parts of the government, in what contexts, and with what constraints? In what setting(s) in the public sphere would such a system be used? Would state and local governments have access to the system? Would the private sector be allowed to use it? What entities within the government or private sector would be allowed to use the system? Who could contribute, view, and/or edit data in the system?

---

[10]In general, the narrower the goals, the simpler and, perhaps, less controversial a system is likely to be, although even a narrowly focused system can run into function creep and problems associated with misidentification.

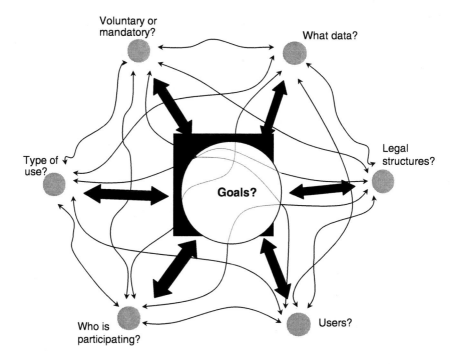

FIGURE 1.1 Interconnecting policy choices. The choices made for each of the questions posed will bear, with differing degrees of influence, on the choices made with respect to all of the other issues. For example, the goals of the system will influence what data are collected about individuals. What data are collected about individuals will constrain the possible goals of the system. Who is allowed to use the system will have a bearing on what legal structures are needed. What legal structures are put in place will bear on what kinds of access to the system are allowed. And so on.

- What *types of use* would be allowed? Who would be able to ask for an ID, and under what circumstances? Assuming that there are datasets associated with an individual's identity, what types of queries would be permitted (e.g., "Is this person allowed to travel?" "Does this person have a criminal record?")? Beyond simple queries, would analysis and data mining of the collected information be permitted? If so, who would be allowed to do this kind of analysis and for what purpose(s)?

- Would participation in and/or identification by the system be *voluntary or mandatory*? In addition, must participants be aware of or consent to having their IDs checked (as opposed to, for example, undergoing surreptitious facial recognition)?

- What *legal structures* would protect the system's integrity, as well as the data subject's privacy and due process rights, and define the government and relying parties' liability for system misuse or failure?

These questions will drive technological considerations (described in Chapter 3), including what kinds and what levels of system security would be required.

Throughout this report, the term "nationwide identity system" is used in lieu of the more colloquial "national ID" or "national ID card." Many of the proposals are often presented in terms of a national identity *card*, though technologies exist—possibly including biometrics, which measures and analyzes unique physiological and behavioral characteristics of individuals—that might serve some of the same proposed purposes without requiring a physical card. Nevertheless, the emphasis in this report is on card-based models simply because they have been proposed most frequently. In addition, many of the policy questions and database-related technical issues apply both to card-based systems and those that do not require a physical card (see Chapter 3).

With respect to the chosen phrase, nationwide identity system, "nationwide" is meant to underscore the scale (both geographic and in terms of numbers of users) needed, without implying that IDs would necessarily be generated from a single central location or, implicit in the term "national," that only citizens would need an ID.

The notion of identity is complicated, even when only the identity of persons (and not things, arguments, systems, etc.) is being referred to, as this report is doing. This report distinguishes between an identifier (the name or sign by which a person is known), which can be thought of as a label by which an individual is known in and to society and with which he or she conducts his or her affairs within society, and the identity of a person as seen by others. For the purposes of this report, "identity" refers to a set of information about a person X believed to be true by Y. More colloquially, identity is associated with an individual as a convenient way to characterize that individual to others. The set of information and the identifier (name, label, or sign) by which a person is known are also sometimes referred to as that person's "identity." The choice of information may be arbitrary, linked to the purpose of the identity verification (also referred to as authentication) in any given context, or linked intrinsically to the person—as in the case of biometrics (see Box 1.1).[11]   For

---

[11]Although biometrics are proposed with increasing frequency for a variety of identification and authentication purposes, they pose many difficult issues for system design, implementation, and use. These will be explored in the committee's final report.

BOX 1.1
Terminology

For the purposes of this brief report, and to help clarify discussion, concepts that the committee's final report[1] will explore in detail are explained here.

- *Identity.* The identity of X according to Y is a set of statements believed by Y to be true about X. In this report, identity generally refers to a set of information about X, especially in the context of a particular identity system.
- *Identification.* Identification is the process of determining to what identity a particular individual corresponds, often without a claimed identity on the part of the individual (for example, the identification of an unconscious patient in an emergency room).
- *ID.* In this report, ID refers to the identity information pertaining to a particular individual that is contained within an identity system and/or the token associated with that information.
- *Authentication.* Authentication is the process of confirming an asserted identity with a specified or understood level of confidence. Note that authentication is quite distinct from identification.
- *Security.* Security refers to a collection of safeguards that ensure the confidentiality of information, protect the integrity of information, ensure the availability of information, account for use of the system, and protect the system(s) and/or network(s) used to process the information. Security is intended to ensure that a system resists (potentially correlated) attacks.
- *Privacy.* The right to privacy is the right of an individual to decide for himself or herself when and on what terms his or her attributes should be revealed.

It should be noted that each of these terms represents a complicated, nuanced, and, in some instances, deeply philosophical topic. The descriptions of these concepts given here are not meant to be definitive, prescriptive, or comprehensive.

---

[1]See <http://www.cstb.org/web/project_authentication> for more information.

---

example, the information corresponding to an identity may contain facts (such as eye color, age, address), capabilities (for example, licensed to drive a car), medical history, financial activity, and so forth. Generally, not all such information will be contained in the same identity, allowing a multiplicity of identities, each of which will contain information relevant to the purpose at hand. In the phrase "nationwide identity system," the word "identity" implies that decisions must be made about what constitutes an identity within a system and that an identity will be established for participants.

A critical question—which goes beyond the scope of this report, but which must be considered in the larger law-enforcement and national-security context—is whether establishing and verifying identity is either necessary or sufficient for achieving any of the desired objectives of the system. It may be that they require collection and analysis of data and/or prospective or retrospective tracking or surveillance, well beyond mere identity verification.[12] Note that even the question of whether to institute collection of data and surveillance is not binary (see Box 1.2).

"System" may be the most important (and heretofore least discussed) aspect of the term "nationwide identity system," because it implies the linking together of many social, legal, and technological components in complex and interdependent ways.   The success or failure of such a system is dependent not just on the individual components, but on the ways they work—or do not work—together. Each individual component could, in isolation, function flawlessly yet the total system fail to meet its objectives.[13]   The control of these interdependencies, and the mitigation of security vulnerabilities and their unintended consequences, would determine the effectiveness of the system.

A nationwide identity system would also consist of more than simply a database, communications networks, card readers, and hundreds of millions of physical ID cards. The system would need to encompass policies and procedures and to take into account security and privacy considerations and issues of scalability, along with human factors and manageability considerations (if the requirements of use prove too onerous or put up too many barriers to meeting the goal of the relying party, that party might try to bypass the system). The system might need to specify the participants who will be enrolled, the users (individuals, organizations, governments) that would have access to the data, the permitted

---

[12]For example, if the goal were to track the activities or whereabouts of an individual to detect illegal activity or suspicious patterns, surveillance of the behavior and activities of said individual would be needed after identification was accomplished. Surveillance might require a warrant or other judicial intervention, depending on the approach taken. If the goal were to detect suspicious activity by previously unsuspected individuals (in order to prevent illegal activity), correlation of surveyed actions would be required after identification and surveillance were accomplished. Such correlation would presumably have to be done before establishment of probable cause for a search in order for it to be useful.

[13]There are examples of this in security mechanisms—for example, where individual techniques to provide additional security interact unexpectedly in such a way as to make the system less secure. Charles Perrow explores the broad concept more thoroughly in *Normal Accidents*, McGraw-Hill, 1986. In addition, the Web site <http://www.safeware-eng.com/software-safety/accidents.shtml> describes the distinction between component failure accidents and system accidents.

BOX 1.2
Degrees of Data Collection and Surveillance

Merely asserting that some data collection or surveillance would occur in a system or that data would be analyzed is insufficient. It is important to determine precisely what is meant or intended by "collection" and "analysis" within an identification system. There are at least five different ways to approach this issue:

- *Little to no data collection.* The only data collected and stored are those needed to establish, at a particular time, an individual's identity within the system (for a predetermined meaning of "identity.")
- *Individual data collection.* Information about an individual's activities and behavior is collected and stored but analyzed only upon request by an authorized agent (for example, a court order).
- *Aggregate data collection.* Behavioral data are aggregated and stored but only analyzed upon request or for a specific purpose. It may or may not be possible to link data to an individual.
- *Aggregate data analysis.* Behavioral data are aggregated and proactively analyzed to search for suspicious or abnormal patterns. Upon an authorized request it may or may not be possible to link data to an individual.
- *Individual data analysis.* Each individual's data are proactively analyzed to check for suspicious or abnormal patterns of behavior, and any such findings are flagged and authorized agents alerted.

uses of the data, and the legal and operational policies and procedures within which the system would operate. In addition, a process would need to be in place to register individuals, manipulate (enter, store, update, search and return) identity information about them, issue credentials (if needed), and verify search requests, among other things. The word "system" suggests the complicated nature of what would be required in a way that the colloquial phrase "national ID card" does not.

It is important to note that a variety of identity systems fit within the scope of what is being discussed in this report. The recent AAMVA proposal[14] to link state motor-vehicle databases is a nationwide identity system. So is the recent proposal to create a traveler ID and database to expedite security checks at airports. Each of these systems could and should be subjected to the kind of analysis and critique described in this

---

[14]See <http://www.aamva.org/> for more information. The committee received a briefing describing some of the issues facing AAMVA in developing a more secure driver's license infrastructure in a context where use of driver's licenses is expanding beyond their nominal function.

report. Some of the issues raised here will be more applicable to some systems than to others, but virtually any large-scale identity system will need to take into consideration a number of policy and technological issues; in fact, before deciding to build any identity system, the issues outlined in this report should be explored.

A top-down, monolithic system controlled by the federal government is not the only kind of nationwide identity system that this report addresses. For example, unifying document formats and linking the databases of state driver's licenses and ID-issuing systems would provide broad (though not complete) coverage without creating a federally controlled nationwide identity system. Further, the successes and failures of the various nationwide identity systems in use in other countries should be examined in order to have a fully informed discussion in the United States. However, when studying such systems, questions of scale must be kept in mind. Experience with a system for a population of tens of millions is not necessarily applicable to a system that might incorporate hundreds of millions. In any case, many of the questions raised in this report assume large-scale systems and widespread participation in and use of such systems.

Without attempting to answer comprehensively the many questions surrounding a nationwide identity system and without making assertions about whether to move toward or away from a nationwide identity system, the report aims to highlight some of the significant policy, procedural, and technical challenges presented by such a system, with the overall goal of prompting a broad discussion among and between policy makers and stakeholders.

This brief document is intended to inform the policy debate. Complete policy analysis is outside its scope, though several of the broad themes outlined here will be addressed more fully in the committee's final report. Chapter 2 describes what the committee believes is the most important issue in the debate—namely, the system goals—along with other policy issues that the committee believes should be considered in advance of implementation and deployment. Chapter 3 explores some of the technological issues involved in implementing a reliable and secure nationwide identity system while minimizing unintended consequences, such as compromises of privacy or the creation of new vulnerabilities. Chapter 4 offers concluding remarks and suggestions.

2

Policy Considerations

Numerous policy questions surround any proposed nationwide identity system. They require sustained deliberation by policy makers and significant input from the various stakeholders—including federal, state, and local governments and agencies, privacy advocates, public-interest groups, civil rights and liberties groups, and those who would participate in and use the system (that is, ID holders, ID requestors, and data analysts). Establishing a nationwide identity system would almost certainly be a complex and expensive process, requiring years of legislative, technical, and public relations work, as systems now in place elsewhere have shown.[1]

WHAT DOES IDENTITY PROVIDE?

Whether and when knowledge of "identity" could aid in solving a problem or meeting an objective depends in part on the word's very definition. For the purposes of this report, identity refers to sets of information (say, a database record or a strongly linked system of records) about a person that can be used to tell who that person is. Confirmation

---

[1]In the Philippines, for example, the social security system ID card project has been under active development and deployment for 6 years and has only reached an enrollment of just over 2 million, en route to the goal of enrolling 40 million social security beneficiaries, members, and dependents.

(at some level of assurance) of identity is useful in contexts when one or more of the following are needed: (1) knowledge (in the present) about a person's past is sought (e.g., the use of a dossier), (2) knowledge about a person in the present needs to be remembered for use in the future (e.g., the creation of a dossier), (3) distinguishing between two individuals is required to prevent the possibility of mistaking one of them for the other, or (4) verification of identity information provided by a third party. Identification and/or authentication are generally used to aid in recognition when there are multiple dealings with a single individual but could also be relevant to a single experience/transaction. (Note that authentication presumes a proffered identity that needs to be confirmed, whereas identification does not—see Box 1.1.)

While casual discussions of IDs or ID cards may assume simple, unique pairings of information and individuals, the reality is often more complicated. In practice, individuals usually have multiple identities—to family, to an employer or school, to neighbors, to friends, to business associates, and so on. Thus, different sets of information are associated with an individual in different contexts—and sometimes an ID card or equivalent is relied upon to provide or point to that information. For identity systems that have existed in our society for some time, there is a common understanding of what information is associated with each. A record associated with a driver's license, for example, includes traffic violations; a record associated with a credit card includes late payment information; and so on.

Multiple identities (that is, multiple sets of information corresponding to a single individual) may allow individuals to control who has access to what kinds of information about them, and the use of multiple identities can be a legitimate strategy for controlling personal privacy in an information society. In addition to providing a measure of privacy protection, the use of multiple identities, even with respect to a single organization, serves legitimate and desirable functions in societal institutions as well. One individual may have several distinct roles with respect to a particular organization. For example, as far as the IRS is concerned, one might be an individual taxpayer, an IRS employee, or the comptroller of a nonprofit organization.

If, however, colluding agents are willing to make the effort, they might be able to link an individual's records—through additional information or correlation with each other's information—to create a single record. In many cases, an identity will include a common cross-reference, such as a Social Security number, that makes it trivially easy to link it to other identities. Moreover, there are usually other possible cross-references (such as address, age, and so on) that enable different sets of information to be linked, though there may be institutional practices or practical barriers that discourage such linking.[2] In addition, questions arise as to how reliable the linking would be—some institutions may not mind if linkages are not completely supported, whereas others demand high levels of accuracy.

Sometimes, the use of multiple identities by a single person, or the use of a single identity by multiple persons, may be evidence of (or exploitable for) fraudulent behavior. Several criminals could use a single identity not considered problematic within the system, or a single terrorist could use the least suspicious of multiple identities accessible to him for boarding a plane. In principle, a nationwide identity system could, in some contexts, eliminate or significantly reduce these sorts of problems if it is designed to prevent both multiple individuals from claiming a single identity and multiple identities from being claimed by a single person.[3]

One implication of the term "national ID" is that these identities are centrally managed in order to make it difficult, if not impossible, for one person to have multiple identities. A system designed to link a person to a single identity (and prohibit use of multiple identities by a single person) within a certain domain must be mandatory (that is, everyone within the domain of interest must be included in the system), otherwise those wishing to establish multiple identities would simply opt out of the program. Also, checking is essential at the time an individual joins, to be sure that he or she is not already in the system. If an identity reveals potentially damaging information about a person, the person may try to avoid the entry of this information into the system by creating a different identity. In some cases, this capability is controlled by having only one central registry for the identity information.[4]

---

[2]See the 1997 CSTB report *For the Record: Protecting Electronic Health Information.*

[3]Historically, the Social Security Administration (SSA) allowed husbands and wives to share a single Social Security number, and some grandfathered couples still do. Thus, such an SSA "identity" refers to two people. Similarly, children and one of their parents can share a single passport and passport number. More commonly, the case of two or more individuals maintaining a joint bank account illustrates one identity (the bank account and associated information) being shared by multiple individuals. Creating multiple identities out of the single record set would be extremely hard for the issuing agencies, because the linked people usually share a single last name. Splitting the record, therefore, might require additional personal information.

[4]A current example of a system that attempts to disallow multiple identities is the Commercial Driver's License Information System (CDLIS). U.S. federal law—the Commercial Motor Vehicle Safety Act of 1986 (P.L. 99-570)—prohibits commercial truck drivers from having multiple driving identities. In compliance with the law, CDLIS is used by the states— via a centralized system that links the various issuing (state) agencies—to check that multiple licenses are not issued. However, nothing in the CDLIS system itself prevents multiple drivers from using this single license and, in fact, fraud of this type has been documented (see "Biometric Identification Standards Research: Final Report Volume I," San Jose State University, December 1997, at <http://www.engr.sjsu.edu/biometrics/fhwabiom.zip>).

Depending on the goals of the system, creating a tight identity-to-individual bond might be excessive. Often it doesn't matter exactly who someone is as long as it is clear that he or she is a member of a particular group (e.g., over 21 or an officer of a corporation with check-signing privileges). Such group identities are often extremely useful in expediting matters in certain contexts and may raise fewer privacy concerns.

Thus, any proposal for a new identity system requires a discussion of what sorts of identity information would be relevant and helpful to the stated goals of the system.[5] It also requires taking into account the levels of confidence with which information was associated to an individual, since basing a system on fragile or unreliable data poses numerous risks. In addition, in some cases there are legal restrictions on what sort of information may be asked of an individual (presumably to include in that person's associated identity information)—for example, it may not be legal to take into account a person's race, gender, national origin, religion, and so forth. In other cases, retaining the advantages that come with the ability of an individual to maintain multiple identities or to maintain group identities could also be desirable. All in all, establishing what is meant by "identity" in a nationwide identity system—in other words, which collection of information is meant to encapsulate an individual's distinctiveness—is a first-order concern.

TO WHOM AND FOR WHAT?

Once the notion of identity has been articulated, a determination must be made as to who would be issued an ID (see Box 1.1 for the distinction between "ID" and "identity") and for what purpose. First and foremost, the goals and requirements of the system must be carefully articulated. What problems should the system be designed to solve? How would it provide solutions to those problems? Without a priori decisions about what types of system functions, determined by policy choices, are desired, the software and hardware may impose unwanted or undesirable restrictions or allowances.[6]

If a goal of the system is the identification and/or tracking of non-U.S. nationals, then issuing IDs only to U.S. citizens would not be sufficient.

---

[5]If the goal of the system is to aid in counterterrorism, then relevant questions might include the following: Is a past criminal record a signal of a potential terrorist? Is a long record of frequent travel a signal that a person is or is not likely to be a terrorist? And so on.

[6]See Lawrence Lessig's treatment of software imposing values in *Code and Other Laws of Cyberspace*, Basic Books, New York, 1999.

Identification and tracking of all individuals would be required.[7] Furthermore, non-U.S. nationals are already required to have IDs when in the United States (passports and, in some cases, visas); however, there is likely to be less control over—and therefore less confidence in—such foreign-issued credentials. This raises questions about international coordination, cooperation, and harmonization.[8,9] The problems now present in keeping track of passports and visas, and in assuring that the right individuals and agencies have the appropriate data when needed, would undoubtedly persist in a new identification system.[10] They also serve to demonstrate how difficult it is to implement a large identification system that is also robust.

What Is Required for ID Issuance?

The best that any system of authentication can do is provide a compelling connection with some previous verification of identity. Accordingly, trust in the integrity of the system is based not so much on the first such verification as on increasing confidence when all previous transac-

---

[7]The terrorist attacks of September 11, 2001, were carried out exclusively by non-U.S. nationals; none of them would have had a U.S. ID if one had been required only of citizens. In addition, undercover operatives sponsored by a major foreign group or state hostile to the United States generally are individuals without suspicious records. It follows that such people's IDs (be they within a United States nationwide identity system or outside it) would not contain anything particularly problematic.

[8]The logistical considerations involved in issuing high-security identities for everyone entering the country are significant, especially when individuals do not need visas in advance (such as citizens of countries in the Visa Waiver Program).

[9]Even if IDs were issued to foreign visitors entering the United States, the information would be based on information provided by their country of origin. Its usefulness is limited for at least two reasons: (1) many countries do not have much data about their citizens to begin with, and others may be unlikely to provide other nations with suspicious background information about their own citizens and (2) even if a country indicates that an individual seeking admission to the United States has a problematic background record, that doesn't mean the United States would consider such a person a risk (for example, a country might provide warnings about political dissidents). Adding information to an individual's ID beyond what his or her country of origin provides (presumably gathered by U.S. intelligence) is problematic for a number of reasons, including cost, scale, paucity of data, and potential compromise of sources and methods behind the information.

[10]As an example of this, the *Washington Post* reported that 15 of the September 11 hijackers applied for visas in Saudi Arabia, where officials have indicated that identity theft is a serious concern. See <http://www.washingtonpost.com/wp-dyn/articles/A14788-2001 Oct30.html>.

tions with that particular individual have worked out.[11] But at the outset, upon determination of who should have IDs, a host of questions arises: How is identity first established within the system? What information would be required of an individual upon application? How would that information be verified?

Such broad questions imply others that are more specific: How would the "true" identity of individuals be established (e.g., for individuals in the initial stages of a program or after card loss or destruction)? What family name(s) would be used for the individual (birth name, adopted name, married name, father's name, father's mother's name)? Could middle names, diminutives, or nicknames be used as first names? When can or must these names be changed? How would people with similar or identical names (or other pieces of associated data) be differentiated in the system? If participation in the system were mandatory, at what point in a person's life would the ID begin to be required? How frequently would renewal be required? Under what circumstances would reissuance be required? What if the system "loses" a person (that is, a person claims to be in the system, but his or her information is not accessible)?

What Is the Meaning of an ID?

Broader, and perhaps more important, is the meaning of the ID (that is, the identity information about a person in the identity system and its associated token). Would the law define rights, privileges, and obligations with respect to the ID? Would the law define a legal person in terms of the ID, or vice versa, or neither? Related to the meaning is the issue of a citizen's and the government's responsibilities with respect to a nationwide identity system. A host of legal issues arises if an ID is to have significance as, say, a government-authorized identification token. Using an ID to verify a person's identity would not be of value without an obligation to present it upon demand by authorities or in an authorized search of one's person.[12]

Questions that would need to be addressed include the following: When must the ID be carried? When must it be presented to a government official? What happens if the holder refuses to present it? What happens if the ID has been lost or stolen? How can information on the ID

---

[11]Although trust developed in this fashion is vulnerable as well. For example, individuals may act in a completely trustworthy fashion for a long period of time and then behave fraudulently or criminally.

[12] Other identification techniques, such as facial recognition, might not require an obligation to present an ID.

(or associated with it) be changed, and by whom? What if the infrastructure is down and the ID cannot be verified? Can only the federal government compel the presentation of the ID, or would state and local government officials (which is where most law-enforcement occurs and many social services are delivered) also have such authority?[13]

Where Does the Identity Information Reside?

These questions point to other questions that must be considered about the information associated with a person's ID. If it is a card or other physical token, what information is stored on it in human-readable format on the ID? What information does the ID store in machine-readable format? What information about or pertaining to an individual is stored in the identity system's databases? What information in those databases is explicitly linked to information in other databases? Who has the authority to create these linkages? Who can access which information about a person in the system? What algorithms are used to analyze data in order to make assessments about a particular individual in a particular context (e.g., risk profiling)?[14]   (See Figure 2.1 for a description of what can happen to identity information within a system.)

Many of the questions raised in this section point more broadly to the problem of controlling function creep (as mentioned in Chapter 1). Decisions and policies made for one kind of system may not apply well if that system begins to be used for other than its original purposes. In the context of an identity system, function creep can occur when the same ID/token is used to access multiple systems. (This has happened with driver's licenses in that they are used not only to prove authorization to drive, but also for proof of age and proof of address in various contexts.)

---

[13]For example, if the goal were to locate and keep track of non-U.S. citizens and/or known criminals within the United States, it would probably be necessary to challenge all individuals (including citizens) to present the card at regular intervals and/or for a wide variety of activities. It would further be necessary to require all individuals to carry the card at all times. It could be that many forms of purchases and transactions would require use of the card in an ancillary fashion, in the same way that purchases with a check often require the presentation of a driver's license or equivalent form of photo identification. In this way, the information associated with the card (and by extension with the holder's identity) would become part of the records generated by some set of interactions, just as Social Security numbers and license numbers are used today—a practice that suggests the development, in effect, of dossiers. A question then arises as to what an individual's failure or refusal to present the card under these circumstances would mean.

[14]The European Data Protection Directive mandates a limited right of individuals to know what algorithms are used to make decisions about them on the basis of personal information.

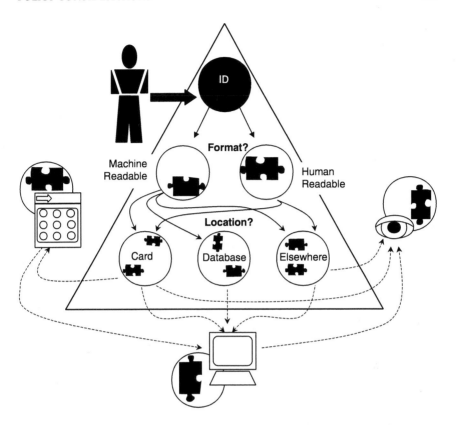

FIGURE 2.1 Potential information flow in identity systems. The information associated with an individual identity could be distributed within the identity system in multiple ways. Parts of it may be machine-readable, parts may be readable by humans. Parts may be stored on a card, in a database, or elsewhere. Access to this information may be available to other systems, card readers, and/ or people. Not present in this diagram, but implicit, is the notion that pieces of information, once outside the system, could then be added to other systems. Or, information from outside the system could be incorporated into this system. Understanding how information flows through the system, who has access to it, and who can change it will be important in understanding both the security and privacy implications of an identity system.

Reuse of an ID/token for purposes beyond the original intent leads to the feasibility of correlating information from many different sources and systems, which can be a cause of concern, particularly with respect to privacy. Strategies and policies that prevent or constrain function creep will be an important factor in any identity system.

PERMITTED USERS OF THE SYSTEM

Another set of policy questions arises over users of a nationwide identity system (recall that a system encompasses numerous social, legal, and technological aspects): May only the government use or request an ID? Under what circumstances? Which branches (federal, state, local) of the government? May any private person or commercial entity request presentation of an ID within the system? May any private person or commercial entity require presentation of an ID? Would certain private-sector organizations be required to use, ask for, and verify IDs? If so, there is a possibility that such mandates might be interpreted as a safe harbor with respect to some liability questions. How would that be handled? Who may use the information on (or associated with) the ID, and for what? Who may enter or modify information associated with the ID?

Depending on the goals of the system, use of the system by the private sector may be necessary. For example, if the goal is to create a database to mine for suspicious activities, tracking of a broad class of activities in the private sector may be viewed as critical. To accomplish this tracking, the ID would need to be presented in connection with many transactions in the private sector (e.g., when traveling on commercial airlines, when purchasing weapons, or when staying in a hotel.) However, as the set of users of a system expands, securing against misuse becomes more complicated. Widespread use (and abuse) of the information associated with an ID is a major concern, underscoring the importance of the initial policy choices related to the purpose of the system.

Management and Operations

Determining how any nationwide identity system should be managed and operated will be a key issue. If the federal government were to play a leading role in operations and management, an overhaul of business and management practices at multiple levels might be necessary.[15] In addition, worldwide coordination would likely be necessary. For ex-

---

[15]Since passage of the Paperwork Reduction Act of 1995, the Office of Management and Budget has been challenged to manage complex information assurance issues, even though it has both budgetary and statutory authority. The Department of Defense, as another example, is charged with managing classified and other national security systems. Nationwide identity systems pose new problems for each of these organizations. If the federal government were to attempt oversight of the system, it would be necessary to determine an appropriate management model suited to undertaking management of large-scale identity systems.

ample, depending on the system goals, ID issuance by U.S. consulates abroad may have to be allowed, raising the potential for fraudulently obtained IDs. Pragmatically, even the most secure documents issued by the U.S. government (passports, green cards, and even currency) have been forged with regularity. Requiring federal government management and operations expertise for nationwide identity systems thus raises a host of issues that must be taken into consideration.

Another set of policy issues involves the roles of the public, private, and not-for-profit sectors in a nationwide identity system. For example, in place of the above scenario (in which the federal government takes responsibility for the management and administration of a nationwide identity system), the private sector alone might develop and maintain the system. Alternatively, the private sector could be subordinate to some procuring federal agency, in which case any resulting data would be subject to federal laws such as the Privacy Act, the Computer Matching Act, the Government Information Security Reform Act, and the Computer Security Act.[16]

Of course, some hybrid model—featuring a public/private partnership—is also possible, though it would require explicit designation of which sector is responsible for what and who might be liable to potentially aggrieved parties when errors or abuses occur. (In particular, careful attention should be paid to due process issues that may arise in connection with error correction.) In any case, it would be absolutely necessary to define how a single organization's private role in enabling the system should relate, if at all, to that same organization's private role in its use. Furthermore, how the private entity would be funded would also be an issue. Moreover, the goals of private institutions with respect to such a system are likely to be very different from those of public institutions.[17] This difference in ultimate objectives could lead to significantly

---

[16]These acts all impose regulatory requirements on federal agencies that collect, use, and maintain sensitive information. The Privacy Act and the Government Information Security Reform Act in particular impose significant public notice and comment requirements on federal agencies to ensure public participation in the appropriateness of planned agency uses of data. The Computer Security Act imposes a risk-based standard for agencies to ensure they protect the confidentiality, integrity, and availability of sensitive federal information and supporting systems. If a nationwide identity system turned out not to be a federal government system, these laws would not apply and the protections they offer would not be available to individuals whose information is housed in the system.

[17]For example, a small-store owner probably is not as interested in customers' individual identities at point-of-sale transactions as he or she is in receiving assurance that payment will be made.

different system requirements and design and could encourage function creep over time.

PERMITTED USES OF THE SYSTEM

A key question about a nationwide identity system is the uses to which the information in it will be put. Will the system be designed to foster consolidation of other (especially federal) databases—or might that be a predictable side effect? Will it be designed to support individualized queries about individuals or provide a yes/no answer to simple questions (for example, "Is this individual a U.S. citizen?")? Will the system facilitate data mining to establish "suspicious profiles"? If the system is to be used extensively by law enforcement, checks and balances would need to be put in place to prevent misuse of information (for example, constraints should be placed on how information collected or seen—perhaps tangentially—as a result of a particular investigation can be used for other purposes).

Consider the system's potential need to make real-time associations of persons with identity—a policy question with technology-challenging implications. For many purposes, the linkage between the person and the identity need not be provided instantly. An application for a mortgage need not be processed in seconds. On the other hand, an identity that authorizes access to a secure building must be validated at the time of the intended entry. A related issue is the prospect of constant real-time correlation and analysis of an individual's national-identity-based transactions.[18] It is likely that such correlation, while possibly desirable depending on the goals of the system, would be financially, technologically, and administratively impossible. For that matter, even retrospective correlation of all transactions would be extremely challenging and expensive. Depending on what information must be tracked and stored, very large amounts of data may be generated. And the analysis of large amounts of data while looking for certain kinds of patterns is a large and open research area.

An additional correlation concern relates to potential uses beyond those associated with public safety and counterterrorism. If private entities are allowed to use the nationwide identity system for their own purposes, it is likely that IDs would be linked to a wide range of information, including bank accounts, credit cards, airline tickets, car rentals, hotel stays, retail transactions, purchases of controlled items (guns, explosives,

---

[18]For example, it may be useful to correlate instantly the renting of a large truck in one state with the purchase of a large amount of fertilizer a day later in another state.

perhaps some fertilizers, prescription drugs subject to abuse), phone lines, cell phone accounts, prepaid cell phones, and so on.[19] Even if the data were not explicitly tied together by organizations, linking users by data items in their identity (such as SSNs) is possible. In addition, systems that employ biometrics could have the ability to link individuals whose information is stored in different databases. That is, two different digital representations of an iris or fingerprint could be compared to see if they might have come from the same eye or finger.[20,21]

Finally, privacy is of serious concern to many, especially when information linkages extend across the boundaries of multiple identities—for example, in the linking of health data, credit ratings, or organizational memberships with our employment records. Of greatest concern to most people is the creation without authorization of such linkages by others, particularly those in positions of authority—governments or employers, for example.

The "minimization principle" is often used as a guideline when building systems sensitive to privacy concerns.[22] It relates to the kind and quantity of information collected from and/or about individuals and emphasizes the need to collect only the minimum amount necessary for

---

[19]The issues become even thornier when one considers the possibility that physical items may eventually have their own tracking systems embedded in them. Cross-correlation of information about things *and* people would likely result in an exponential explosion of data, further complicating the technical questions and confounding the privacy issues. See Charlie Schmidt's "Beyond the Bar Code," *Technology Review*, March 2001.

[20]Systems that will allow eye/finger versus database comparisons but not database versus database comparisons have been proposed, such as in N.K. Ratha, J.H. Connell, and R.M. Bolle, "Enhancing Security and Privacy in Biometrics-Based Authentication Systems," *IBM Systems Journal*, vol. 40, No. 3, 2001. Another possible solution would be to use biometrics only at three points in any given system: when checking for duplicate enrollments at initial registration to prevent issuance of multiple IDs to a single user, when checking the binding between the cardholder and the card at point-of-service applications, and when reissuing the card. This check, which could occur without revealing the biometric pattern to the holder of the card, would create yet another point in the system where security is needed.

[21]Work done by Latanya Sweeney (see <http://sweeney.heinz.cmu.edu/confidentiality. html>) suggests that very little information is needed to uniquely identity a particular individual in even an ostensibly anonymized database, suggesting that creating linkages between databases—even without biometric data tying individuals to their data—may not be difficult.

[22]This notion is articulated in a report of the U.S. Privacy Protection Study Commission, *Personal Privacy in an Information Society*, Government Printing Office, Washington, D.C., 1977, also known as the Privacy Commission Report. Three principles espoused in that report are to (1) minimize intrusiveness, (2) maximize fairness, and (3) create legitimate, enforceable expectations of confidentiality.

the desired transaction. Minimization also implies that disclosure of information should be limited to the purpose(s) for which it was collected. A pragmatic reason for this, in addition to the privacy aspects, is that information is likely to have an accuracy commensurate with its original purpose (for example, the address given on a video-store membership application form is more likely to be false than the home telephone number given on an employment application). In addition, the minimization principle suggests that information should be deleted when no longer needed and that the information disclosed be limited to that which is needed to fulfill the request (as opposed to disclosing all available information about an individual or transaction).

Clearly, minimization runs counter to the kinds of information collection and correlation needed for the preemptive and retrospective analyses contemplated by proposals for a nationwide identity system meant to counter terrorism and unlawful activities. Resolving or mitigating this tension will be a serious challenge to those developing policies for a nationwide identity system.

VOLUNTARY OR MANDATORY?

Whether participation in the system is to be required or chosen is a major policy decision. Until the goals of the system are clearly articulated, it will be difficult to gauge which type of participation would be preferable. Some goals may directly or indirectly require mandatory checking of identities and/or enrollment in the system. For example, if the goal were to prohibit travel by persons with malicious intentions, all air travelers would need to be enrolled—if enrollment were voluntary, such people would simply not enroll and would be permitted to travel. In general, any attempt to ascertain that an individual does not possess an unwanted attribute (for example, malicious intent) requires a complete knowledge of behaviors related to that attribute, and hence mandatory checks.

Clearly, a voluntary system is likely to meet with less resistance and to raise fewer concerns about civil liberties, although its voluntary nature would seem to limit the kinds of goals that it could expect to achieve. However, even when a system is nominally voluntary, attention should be paid to whether the large inconveniences of nonparticipation make it effectively mandatory. Deliberate consideration of whether and when to require participation and the implications of widespread but voluntary participation would be essential.

There are at least two levels at which participation occurs: when an individual establishes an identity within the system and when his or her ID is requested or used in a given interaction. Whether an individual must consent to presenting his or her ID as opposed to having the ID observed from a distance (possibly without the person's knowledge) is another critical policy decision.

WHAT LEGAL STRUCTURES?

In considering whether to implement any nationwide identity system, decision makers would have to determine whether and how such a system would be regulated, and by whom. What constitutes misuse of the ID or the data associated with it? What penalties are imposed on the holder for misusing or tampering with the ID? What penalties are imposed on officers of the government for abuse of the card or misuse of its information? What penalties are imposed on private parties or businesses other than the holder for abuse of the card or misuse of the identity and associated information? Would laws permit, discourage, or forbid private-sector actors from asking individuals to present the card for reasons other than those intended by the public sector?

Depending on the policy choices and deployment strategies a nationwide identity system reflects, its constitutional implications may be significant. The constitutional limitations on an agent's ability to require presentation of IDs,[23] along with the limitations on the ability of Congress to enact a nationwide identity system, should be explored before any such enactment to avert the costs of imposing the system and then having to revise or abandon it in the face of its unconstitutionality, to say nothing of its effects on civil liberties.

Depending on implementation details and policy decisions, a nationwide identity system could be used to compile and store large amounts of information on individuals, so that the legal restrictions on compiling and using dossiers would have to be strictly obeyed. More broadly, an understanding of the principles that support significant privacy-related authorities, as well as the major legal traditions and principles that drive U.S. privacy law and policy, will be necessary when considering identity systems that will handle personally identifiable information.[24] In particular,

---

[23]In fact, the Supreme Court has limited the situations in which government authorities and police officers may require individuals to leave an area due to lack of apparent purpose. See *Brown v. Texas* at <http://caselaw.lp.findlaw.com/cgi-bin/getcase.pl?navby=case&court=us&vol=443&invol=47>.

[24]U.S. Department of Health, Education and Welfare, Secretary's Advisory Committee on Automated Personal Data Systems, *Records, Computers, and the Rights of Citizens*, Government Printing Office, Washington, D.C., 1973.

it would be helpful to have insight into the statutory models that pertain where mistakes can have severe repercussions (such as census information collection or tax returns).

A further consideration is that because identification in the form of birth certificates and driver's licenses has traditionally been done at the state and local level, states' rights and associated issues could well arise. It will be important to examine the federal/state constitutional tensions along with how such issues may facilitate or impede development of policy solutions in this arena. How, for example, should a nationwide identity system interact with the other federal, state, and local identity systems that are already in place? Should these other systems continue, be coupled to the nationwide system, or be superseded?

BENEFITS AND DRAWBACKS

Creation of a well-thought-out and well-designed nationwide identity system could have some advantages over the current methods of establishing and verifying identity, such as state-issued driver's licenses, Immigration and Naturalization Service documents, and birth certificates. Current systems have many characteristics that pose a challenge to meeting the goals expressed by proponents of a more uniform nationwide identity system. For example, the documents in current systems are not standardized in form or information content, so that a person inspecting an offered document often cannot determine if it even *resembles* an authentic document (much less whether it actually *is* authentic) without substantial research.

Similarly, such documents are generally not strongly linked to the person who offers one for identity, allowing several people to use a single authentic document. Identities also cannot be clearly revoked in current systems, allowing a person to successfully offer an invalid ID as verification of identity. Moreover, these systems do not universally employ strong anticounterfeiting measures—indeed, the existing measures vary from document to document, and the documents are not easily checked.

A nationwide identity system, depending on its implementation, might drive many other forms of identification out of use by subsuming their functionality. Several factors in particular could encourage widespread third-party reliance on the nationwide identity system to the exclusion of current systems. First, if the cost of the system is borne by the government and its associated agencies, the system's use would be free to other segments of society unless measures (technical, legal, or otherwise) are taken to prevent unauthorized use. Second, unless private parties are prevented by law (or restrictions on technology) from relying on the nationwide identity system, the liability associated with such reliance would be shielded by the government's sovereign immunity. Third, even if the private parties were forbidden to rely on the data, it is very likely that private commercial organizations would begin to correlate data about citizens based on their card and/or identity within the system. The information in these commercial databases may not be as strongly protected (legally or technologically) as, presumably, is the information in the nationwide identity system's own databases. The correlation and aggregation of personal information thus raise a variety of policy questions about the use of such information and constraints on it.

As Garrett Hardin wrote in 1968, "You can't do just one thing."[25] The introduction of a nationwide identity system would create ripples throughout society and the legal system. It is difficult to predict what unintended effects these ripples would have. In part due to our frontier history, there seems to be a widespread belief in our country that some socially good things derive from the current inability to strongly correlate an identity with an individual—for example, a person often has the option of leaving some detail of his or her life behind. Examples include the expunging of the criminal records of minors, anonymous testing for sexually transmissible diseases (and the consequent public-health benefits of reducing the incidence of these diseases), shielding the identity of rape victims from public view, and erasing the records of bankruptcy after a statutory interval.

It is not known how much the smooth operation of society depends on such things, or on the assumption that they are possible. There is a risk, however, that they would be lost, or at least significantly impaired, if a broadly used nationwide identity system came into existence.[26] Ensuring the privacy protections in these examples would likely depend on carefully limiting access to, and the specific uses of, the system's databases, and on restricting the required uses of an ID to certain circumstances.

Identity theft is already a critical problem,[27] even without central-

---

[25]Garrett Hardin, "The Tragedy of the Commons," *Science* 162:1243-1248 (1968).

[26]Years of experience show that when people automate or regiment a previously manual or only lightly regimented system, they discover the new system's demand that things be done "exactly right" can create havoc, and that what used to be a smooth process needs to be redesigned to accommodate the less flexible automated system. Decision makers must consider that introducing a rigorous identity system might wreak similar havoc when people discover that some authentication activities require more flexibility than the new system can offer.

[27]*Time* magazine notes that in 2001 the "Federal Trade Commission logged more than 85,000 complaints from people whose identities had been pirated" and that "some consumer advocates suggest as many as 750,000 identities are stolen each year." See <http://www.time.com/time/nation/article/0,8599,196857,00.html>.

ized, mandated identities for everyone. Identity theft is an individual's fraudulent claim that he or she is the person to whom the information in the system refers, allowing him or her to derive some benefit from another party who is relying on that claim. It might involve theft of a physical ID token or it might involve the thief's learning some secret or personal information and using this in lieu of the token. One reason for the problem is the broad misuse of SSNs, coupled with the fact that the number itself is small enough to be easily memorized. In addition, birth and death data in the United States are not subject to stringent accuracy requirements nor are they highly correlated, making it relatively straightforward to exploit a deceased person's birth certificate in order to establish credentials as a basis for an identity.

Given the attendant risks, a nationwide identity system would need to provide much better protection against identity theft than do current systems of identification.[28] Additional questions arise in the context of a nationwide system of how to recover from identity theft. Who would have the authority to restore or create a new identity for someone when necessary? And what safeguards would be needed to prevent this authority from being abused?

While offering better solutions to some problems surrounding identity theft, a nationwide identity system poses its own risks. For example, it is likely that the existence of a single, distinct source of identity would create a single point of failure that could facilitate identity theft. The theft or counterfeiting of an ID would allow an individual to "become" the person described by the card, in very strong terms, especially if the nationwide identity system were to be used for many purposes other than those required by the government. Paradoxically, it could be that a robust nationwide identity system makes identity theft more difficult while at the same time making its consequences more dire. The economic incentive to counterfeit these cards could turn out to be much greater than the economic incentive to counterfeit U.S. currency.

---

[28]One strategy might be for the system to avoid displaying human-readable ID "numbers" or other unique identifiers to private organizations. This would, in effect, make it impossible for anyone to read another person's information off his or her card. (Imagine, for example, a credit card that does not have the account number embossed on the front but makes it available only to machines that read magnetic stripes, thereby reducing opportunities for casual theft). The strategy would instead require that agents use cryptographic techniques to authenticate individuals or enable transactions. See Figure 2.1 for a description of the kinds of information in an identity system and where the information might end up.

To determine what safeguards are necessary, a realistic threat analysis would be required. Are the as-yet-undetermined countermeasures up to the challenge? Any proposed system must be examined to determine whether the net result with respect to identity theft would be better or worse than it is now. It may be that more robust security in a nationwide identity system, along with increased attention to data integrity (for example, correlating birth and death records, as discussed above) in current identity systems, would mitigate some of the identity theft problems that arise.

3

Technological Challenges

Though the aim of this short report is merely to point out some of the essential policy questions that would be raised by the introduction of a nationwide identity system, the committee believes that the technological and implementation challenges raised—even without a precise characterization of such a system's goals or subsequent policies—are enormous and that they warrant significant and serious analysis.

This need becomes clear when an ID is understood as an element of a much larger system that includes technical, material, and human elements. At a minimum,

- Cards and card readers (if used for validation) would need to be designed, fabricated, distributed, and updated or otherwise maintained or replaced.
- A corresponding (backend) database would need to be established, maintained, and protected.
- Procedures for checking the authenticity of IDs and for verifying the presenter (with or without specialized equipment) would need to be established, promulgated, practiced, and audited.[1]

---

[1]Association of an identity card with its holder has to be verified before the identity information it contains can be relied upon (otherwise, stealing the card would permit the theft of the cardholder's identity).

• Means to discover, report, verify, and authoritatively correct mistakes would need to be put in place.

• A variety of security measures would need to be factored into all aspects of the system to be sure that it meets its objectives and is not vulnerable to things such as fraud or denial-of-service abuses that can result in privacy violations.

Fraud (and security in general) is a significant concern in any system, even the most technologically sophisticated.[2] The nationwide scale of such a system would require knowing that all aspects of the system are scalable—a daunting problem for lesser systems.[3] In any case, the challenges of building robust and trustworthy information systems—they are extensive and well-documented[4]—are accompanied by the even greater challenge of making the systems resistant to attacks by well-funded adversaries.

Architectural issues include the degree of centralization of the underlying databases as well as the location and cost of data storage, computation, and communication, which can all be done at different places.[5] For example, how would authorized entities obtain the records they wanted, under what circumstances, and with what degree of authorization? Would there be daily or weekly downloads of selected records to more permanent storage media? Would a real-time network feed be required (perhaps similar to those used in real-time credit authorization systems)? Would it be possible to secure such a feed sufficiently?[6]

Choices among architectural options, as well as other options, would depend on the functional goal(s) of the system. Architecture influences scalability, cost, and usability/human factors. It also interacts with proce-

---

[2]A large breach of security with French banking cards is causing a significant upgrade of the infrastructure in France (<http://parodie.com/english/smart card.htm>). In the United States, satellite-signal theft by smart card fraud is so extensive that it is now the focus of a government sting operation. See Ross Anderson's work on cryptography and security, much of which is available at <http://www.cl.cam.ac.uk/users/rja14/>.

[3]CSTB's 2000 report *Making IT Better* underscores the profound challenges associated with large-scale systems.

[4]See the CSTB reports *Computers at Risk* (1990), *Trust in Cyberspace* (1999), *Making IT Better* (2000), and *Embedded, Everywhere: A Research Agenda for Networked Systems of Embedded Computers* (2001).

[5]A general rule is that the lower the cost of accessing an online database and the larger the likelihood of doing so, the less sophisticated the card needs to be.

[6]Such security might require a very large new network that would have to be connected *inside* the firewalls of the institutions and organizations using the system. Securing such a network is extremely difficult; experience suggests that maintaining that security would be very challenging.

dure: Decisions must be made about who would be in charge of issuing, reissuing, renewing, revoking, and administering the cards, along with maintaining, updating, and granting access to the database. A further concern is the need for graceful recovery from failure as well as substitute mechanisms when the system is compromised or not adequately responsive at the time verification of an identity is needed. All of these factors influence cost, as well as effectiveness.

Cost needs to be analyzed completely, on a life-cycle basis and with attention to numerous trade-offs. Even if software and hardware costs are minimized, experience with lesser systems—from SSNs to state drivers' licenses to military identification systems—shows that there will be significant ongoing administrative costs for training, issuing cards, verification, maintenance (keeping whatever information is associated with an individual and his or her ID up to date), and detection and investigation of counterfeiting.[7] In particular, the costs—and technological and administrative complexity—of assuring the integrity and security of an identity infrastructure are likely to be large. They would depend in part on whether technology for automated checking of an ID—as opposed to a visual check used today with SSNs or drivers' licenses—is required, which in turn depends on the choice of ID technology (see Box 3.1).

For example, in response to legislation enacted in August 1996,[8] the Social Security Administration (SSA) conducted an analysis and produced a report on options for enhancing the Social Security card.[9] Citing a number of key business and technology assumptions that appeared valid at the time of the study (1997), SSA estimated that issuing enhanced cards might have a life-cycle cost of $5.2 billion to $10.5 billion, depending on the technology developed and deployed. These estimates included assumptions about the need for reissuing cards, issuing new cards, and maintaining the systems in order to store data related to the cards and keep that data up to date. The study did not assume that each SSN and its related card would relate to just one individual, because SSA estimated that at the time, approximately 10 million of the 269 million valid SSNs

---

[7]There are numerous ways in which fraudulent ("novelty") identification documents can be obtained. A simple Web search on "fake id" provides links to many possible suppliers.

[8]Section 111 of P.L. 104-193, "Personal Responsibility and Work Opportunity Reconciliation Act of 1996" (Welfare Reform) and section 657 of P.L. 104-208, Division C, "Illegal Immigration Reform and Immigrant Responsibility Act of 1996" (Immigration Reform).

[9]See *Report to Congress on Options for Enhancing the Social Security Card*, Social Security Administration, Publication No. 12-002, September 1997. Available at <http://www.ssa.gov/history/reports/ssnreport.html>.

were duplicates (that is, two or more persons had been given the same SSN). There was a variety of reasons for such duplication, including error on the part of SSA and malfeasance on the part of some individuals.

As with the design of any system, decisions about trade-offs would need to be made in advance. The security, efficiency, and effectiveness options chosen would depend on the goals and policies (see Chapter 2) and the planned uses of the system. For example, a "trusted traveler" system whose sole function was to authenticate individuals who had been previously certified as "trusted" in the particular context of travel might place more emphasis on efficiency in travel-related queues and on eliminating false positives than on protecting the fact that a particular person has been certified as trusted (or untrusted). A secure driver's license system, in which the license is used as an ID for many activities beyond driving on a public roadway, might trade ease of replacing a lost license against the rigorous authentication of individuals who request a replacement. In making decisions about trade-offs, understanding the potential threats and risks will be a large component of assessing the security requirements of a system.

BINDING PERSONS TO IDENTITIES

A practical issue that would arise in a card-based identity system is that of relating cards and identities to individuals: How would the issuing authorities create this binding? Most of the systems (both hypothetical and actual) alluded to in this report employ what is known as two-factor authentication, requiring the holders to present more information than the card itself (perhaps a face that matches the picture, a PIN, or a thumbprint) to verify that they are the legitimate holders.

If someone has a valid card, how would anyone know that it belongs to him or her? A picture on the front of the card would not be sufficient if very high assurance is sought.[10] If the card makes use of a magnetic stripe, it would have been easy to copy the stored information to a new card with a different picture. If the card is a memory card or smart card, duplication, while a little more difficult, would still have been possible. If biometric information[11] is used, it could have been stored on the card and

---

[10]The inability of human inspectors to reliably match faces to cards was demonstrated in Pike, Kemp, and Brace, "Psychology of Human Face Recognition," IEEE Conference on Visual Biometrics, London, March 2, 2001.

[11]There are a number of biometrics that might be used; for the purposes of this discussion, assume an iris scan or fingerprint.

BOX 3.1
Cards and Their Requirements

The presumed goal of a counterfeit-resistant, long-lasting, easily replaceable ID presents difficult technical challenges. With respect to the ID itself, assuming that it is a physical artifact such as a card, a number of questions need to be answered.[1] Form factors—the size, shape, and substance of the card—would likely play a part both in acceptance on the part of the citizenry and in the card's resistance to counterfeiting. The more difficult challenges pertain to the aspects of cards that are determined by the kind of technology used.

One could use a relatively simple card, like a credit card or driver's license. Each individual in the system would have a card with some information printed on it about the holder and perhaps a picture. There might be a unique number on the card, and the information in a nationwide database would be indexed by that number. The card itself might contain a magnetic stripe along with embossed and printed data. As with a driver's license or passport, access to this database (for reading data out or putting data in) would presumably be limited,[2] as it would be under the proposal by the American Association of Motor Vehicle Administrators to create nationwide standards for driver's licenses.

On the other hand, the counterfeiting of magnetic stripe cards is a trivial undertaking.[3] More important, the ease with which the information contained in the magnetic stripe can be duplicated means that a counterfeiter can produce a clone card and/or retransmit the data in other transactions as if they came from a legitimate card. All of this implies serious security and privacy vulnerabilities, and there is no verifiable connection (by means of biometrics, for example) between the holder of the card and the person to whom the card was issued. Hence, using such credentials as a basis for issuing new cards (and, ergo, identities) would compromise the accuracy of some of the identification data, inasmuch as the credentials depend on attestations by the individual or even third parties.[4]

---

[1] The Department of Defense is now deploying a smart card that it refers to as a common access card (CAC) as an authentication device and for other purposes. The card combines a magnetic stripe, bar code, a photo ID, and smart card technology. DOD's experiences may well prove instructive when considering a nationwide system. However, the privacy concerns of military employees are likely to be different from those of average citizens, making an exact analogue unlikely. In addition, the CAC will be deployed for a population that is more than an order of magnitude smaller than the U.S. population, which is more diverse in many dimensions than the military and currently less subject than the military to sanctions for failure to comply with the identification system's requirements.

[2] On November 2, 2001, the *Washington Post* reported that the American Association of Motor Vehicle Administrators was working on a plan to link all driver databases and to strengthen the security and functionality of current driver's licenses and state identification cards. See <http://www.washingtonpost.com/wp-dyn/articles/A32717-2001Nov2.html>. See also <http://www.aamva.org/standards/stdAAMVADLIstandard2000.asp> for a description of AAMVA's standard, which aims to provide a uniform means for identifying holders of driver's licenses throughout North America.

[3] See, as just two of many examples, "Skim Artists Can Swipe Your Credit," at <http://www.techtv.com/cybercrime/internetfraud/story/0,23008,2583624,00.html> and "Newly Discovered Bug Skims Credit Card Data," at <http://www.newsfactor.com/perl/story/11494.html>.

[4] Note that the existing identification infrastructure (including the system of birth and death records) in the United States often depends on the presentation of credentials and is highly decentralized. The lack of common national standards generates skepticism about the quality of the data.

Another possibility is a memory card (or storage card), which would hold more information and be more expensive than the magnetic-stripe cards of the previous example.[5] These cards contain memory as well as some security logic to prevent unauthorized reading or tampering with their data. The information contained on them could be digitally signed (that is, a number would be associated with that information that is dependent on a secret known only to the signer as well as on the data itself) to prevent easy counterfeiting. The correspondence between the user and the card (along with the information on the card and in the database) could be ascertained through biometric authentication, which would be undertaken using special equipment—such as a reader for fingerprints or iris scans—in addition to presentation of the card. An additional possibility is to use smart card technology that permits computation (such as digital signatures and encryption) to take place on the card itself.

Though successful attacks have taken place, these cards are even harder to counterfeit than memory cards. They might have a name, photo, number, and biometric data, all of which could be cryptographically signed. The data would be backed up in a database to enable checking when reissuing a card and checking for duplicates when the card is first issued. A card of this sort could engage in a real-time, cryptographic exchange with an online system to verify a user's identity—possibly without exposing details of that identity to the organization performing the data capture—for example, an airline or a retail establishment.

As an example of a card-based system using biometrics, consider the Connecticut Department of Social Services, which issues cards to aid welfare recipients.[6] Fingerprints of each applicant are taken and compared with the fingerprint of all applicants previously enrolled. Under the assumption that people are not modifying their fingerprints (and assuming no matching errors), this can prevent a single user from registering under multiple identities within the system. The card is printed with the fingerprints encoded in a two-dimensional optical bar code on the front of the card. At point-of-service applications, the user presents a fingerprint that is compared with that encoded on the card. This prevents multiple users from making use of a single identity. Other biometric technologies, such as iris recognition, might be useful in this application as well. However, no biometric technology is completely invulnerable to attacks by sophisticated adversaries.[7,8]

---

[5] One example is the INSPASS and the data stored on it, coupled with a hand-geometry reader at point of entry to verify identity. Another example is a German identification card, *die Karte*, which uses two separate smart card chips and contains 22 separate mechanisms for card validation/antifraud technology.

[6] For a discussion of the costs associated with identification cards and fingerprints in social service applications, see "A Review of Five Cost/Benefit Studies of Fingerprinting in Social Service Applications," Roger Salstrom, Burton Dean, and James Wayman, available at <http://www.dss.state.ct.us/digital/news22/bhsug22.htm>.

[7] T. van der Putte and J. Keuning, "Biometrical Fingerprint Recognition: Don't Let Your Fingers Get Burned," *Proceedings of IFIP TC8/WG8.8 Fourth Working Conference on Smart Card Research and Advanced Applications*, Kluwer Academic Publishers, September 2000, pp. 289-303. Also, see T. Matsumoto et al., "Impact of Artificial 'Gummy' Fingers on Fingerprint Systems," *Proceedings of the SPIE*, vol. 4677 (January 2002) and D. Maio, D. Maltoni, J. Wayman, and A. Jain, "FVC2000: Fingerprint Verification Competition 2000," *Proceedings of the 15th International Conference on Pattern Recognition*, Barcelona, September 2000, available on-line at <http://bias.csr.unibo.it/FVC2000/>.

[8] D. Willis and M. Lee, "Six Biometric Devices Point the Finger at Security," *Network Computing*, June 1, 1998.

a "live capture" of the biometric could be carried out when an individual presents the card. The captured data would then be compared with the data stored on the card. Depending on what kinds of cryptographic protections are used, this system could be susceptible to forgery as well—for example, someone might recreate the card with his or her own biometric information in combination with another person's identity information.

Another scenario might be to have the person present a biometric to a controlled scanner and present the card that contains reference information. Both pieces of information are then validated in combination against a backend server. However, this creates a requirement for high availability (that is, the system should be usable essentially all of the time) and a dependence on reliable, secure network and communications infrastructures.

In principle, a card coupled with biometrics and the appropriate infrastructure for reading and verifying biometric data may offer the greatest confidence with respect to linking persons and their cards. But getting biometrics technology right (including control of the risks of compromise) and widely distributed is not easy.[12,13] There are additional issues associated with the use of biometrics, such as some popular resistance.[14]

Note that biometrics allows for cardless system options: A database-only system based solely on biometrics eliminates the risk of card loss or theft, but real-time database accessibility then becomes a major consideration. In addition, compromise of the database is an even greater concern than in card-based systems, where the cards can be used to provide a check against corrupted data in the database. Further, a cardless system implies that anyone wishing to use the system (even for activities needing only moderate to low levels of security) would have to invest in the equipment needed to access the infrastructure in real time.

---

[12]"Advice on the Selection of Biometric Products: Issue 1.0," (U.K.) Communication Electronic Security Group, November 23, 2001, available at <http://www.cesg.gov.uk/technology/biometrics>.

[13]J.D.M. Ashbourn, *Biometrics: Advanced Identity Verification: The Complete Guide,* Springer, London, 2000.

[14]For further information, see the recent RAND report *Army Biometric Applications: Identifying and Addressing Sociocultural Concerns,* 2001. In addition, an accuracy issue arises with biometrics because it uses what are known as probabilistic measures of similarity. No two images of the same biometric pattern (even fingerprints) from the same person are exactly alike. Consequently, biometrics is based on pattern-matching techniques that return sufficiently close measures of similarity. With enough (or not enough) information about the application environment and user population, it is possible to convert those measures into probabilities of a match or nonmatch. Thus, incorrect decisions occur randomly with a probability that can be measured.

Cryptographic protection and digital signatures, in combination with offline verification of the signature and a properly deployed public key infrastructure (PKI),[15] could provide a measure of protection for the information associated with IDs and guard against misuse. But for any technology, some degree of imperfection will exist. Therefore, it is necessary to decide on thresholds for false rejection rates (false negatives) and false acceptance rates (false positives), not only for when the ID is used but also at the time of issuance, reissuance, and renewal. Policy decisions—perhaps with corresponding legal backing—need to be made about what happens in the event of a false negative or false positive. Creation of exception-handling procedures for dealing with incorrect decisions opens up additional vulnerabilities for the system, as impostors might claim to have been falsely rejected and request handling as an exception.

BACKEND SYSTEMS

Once methods are in place to satisfactorily link persons to IDs, the requirements and goals of the system should drive decision making about associated databases. The databases' principal features are likely to include an ability to search based on an ID number or other unique identifier, various ID attributes, and possibly biometric data. Depending on whether tracking and prediction are requirements of the system, significant logging, auditing, and data mining capabilities would be needed as well.

Key issues related to this part of the system stem from both structural and procedural decisions. If the database needs to be readily accessible from remote locations (which is likely), it would almost certainly need to be replicated. This, in combination with its perceived (and actual) value and the fact that more people over a more widespread area would be likely to have authorized access to the system, makes it even more vulnerable to break-ins: by physically accessing one of the sites, by finding some communications-based vulnerability, or by bribing or corrupting someone with access to the system. Moreover, if verification of identity required an online database query at airports, a handful of "accidents" at key places around the country (such as wires being cut at critical points in a way that appears accidental) could cripple civil aviation and any other

---

[15]The committee's final report will examine PKI and other authentication technologies in detail.

commerce that required identity verification (for example, purchase of guns or certain chemicals).

Note that availability would be a key aspect of any online component of a nationwide identity system. While the desire for cost savings might lead to such a backend system being accessible via the public Internet (as opposed to a dedicated network), this would expose the system to yet more attacks, both direct and indirect, on shared infrastructure, such as the routing systems and hardware, the domain name system, or shared bandwidth. As noted previously, it has proven extremely difficult to secure systems that utilize the Internet; a nationwide identity system would likewise need to be widely accessible and would inevitably be the target of malicious attacks as well as subject to unintentional or incidental damage. Failure modes of the system would have to be very carefully studied, and backup plans and procedures would have to be designed and tested for all critical systems that depend on use of the nationwide identity system.

A further complication would result if it were decided that different users should be granted different levels of access to the database, whether for aggregated data or information about individuals. This raises query capability, access control, and security issues. Related to the size of the user base (that is, those who use the identity system to make some sort of determination about an individual) is the question of whether the same security measures need to hold for each user. For example, if the system were used broadly in the private sector, a clerk at a liquor store might be relatively less concerned about detecting counterfeit cards than would be an intelligence or law-enforcement agent granting access to national security-related sites or information. In addition, the clerk would need less information (for example, age of individual is greater than 21) verified through the system than would the agent.

It is a significant challenge to develop an infrastructure that would allow multiple kinds of queries, differing constraints on queries (based on who was making them), restrictions on the data displayed to what was needed for the particular transaction or interaction, and varying thresholds for security based on the requirements of the user. Determining the scope of use and the breadth of the user population in advance would dictate which functionalities are needed.

A further challenge resulting from a wide variety of users and uses is data integrity. Different users (even if the system were used only by agencies within the government) would undoubtedly have different perceptions of how critical the accuracy of the data is. Therefore, to maintain the quality of the data, controls over who could input data, and with what degree of specificity and security, must also be a factor in the design of the system.

Another necessary component of system and data integrity is auditing capability. Keeping track of who has accessed what parts of the system and which data would be necessary for reasons of technology (to track down errors and bugs, for example) and liability.[16]

Procedurally, such a large system would require many people to be authorized to maintain and administer it. Even if perfect technological security were achievable, there would still be the security risk of compromised insiders, given the very large numbers of people needed to maintain and administer the system.[17,18] The human factor would also be an issue with regard to data entry and possible errors in the database. This is well known among statisticians, and various technical and procedural steps can be taken to offset risks of inaccuracy. In general, therefore, correction mechanisms would need to be created; however, these mechanisms provide additional opportunity for fraud. Given the uses to which such a system is expected to be put, however, and potential impacts on individuals' reputations and freedom to function as social and economic actors, mechanisms that allow individuals to know what is in the database and to contest and/or correct alleged inaccuracies would be desirable and politically essential (and, if run by the federal government, legally required). While such mechanisms can be found in credit-reporting and medical databases,[19] the law-enforcement and national-security frameworks that are motivating proposals for a nationwide identity system pose unique accessibility and disclosure challenges.

Another concern is that depending solely on feedback from participants to correct inaccuracies would catch only a fraction of the errors. People may tend to notice and report only those errors that interfere with something they are attempting to accomplish. An incorrectly entered birth date, for example, may not be noticed or corrected for decades and may only come to light when the person applies for, say, Medicare. An

---

[16]Indeed, major federal agencies such as the Internal Revenue Service have run into problems with tracking and controlling access to information. For a discussion of this as it relates to privacy, see Peter P. Swire, "Financial Privacy and the Theory of High-Tech Government Surveillance," *Washington University Law Quarterly* 177(2):461-512 (1999).

[17]CSTB held a planning meeting on the topic of the insider threat in late 2000. For more information, see <http://www.cstb.org/web/whitepaper_insiderthreat>.

[18]The President's Commission on Critical Infrastructure Protection at <http://www.ciao.gov/PCCIP/PCCIP_Report.pdf> discusses cyberthreats, including the insider threat. *Fortune* has examined the cost of insider attacks online at <www.fortune.com/sitelets/sections/fortune/tech/2001_01esecurity2.html>.

[19]See, for example, Computer Science and Telecommunications Board, *For the Record: Protecting Electronic Health Information*, National Academy Press, Washington, D.C., 1997.

accumulation of latent errors is inevitable and leads to at least two problems: (1) by the time the error is discovered it may be hard to locate the information needed to verify the claim of error and (2) the act of making the correction may interfere with or delay some action that should be allowed by the system. Creating a workable nationwide identity system that can compensate in effective ways for these inevitabilities is clearly a nontrivial task.

DATA CORRELATION AND PRIVACY

A key question about a nationwide identity system database is whether it would be designed to foster consolidation of other (especially federal) databases—or whether that might happen as a side effect. Either way, proponents note that this would make information sharing among intelligence and law-enforcement agencies easier,[20,21] although the committee believes that it could also carry significant risks.

A centralized, nationwide identity system essentially offers adversaries a single point of failure and presents an attractive target for identity theft and fraud. The more valuable the information in the database and the credentials associated with an identity, the more they become a target for subversion. Unauthorized access might be sought by terrorists, stalkers, abusive ex-spouses, blackmailers, or organized crime. Furthermore, to the extent that important activities become dependent on the system, the system becomes an attractive target for denial-of-service attacks. Implementing a secure and reliable nationwide identity system that is resistant to credential theft or loss,[22] fraud, and attack is a significant technological challenge, with ancillary procedural challenges.

Related to consolidation, information *correlation* is facilitated by systems in which one individual has exactly one identity. This has both negative and positive implications. Such a system is useful for predicting

---

[20]A forthcoming CSTB report will explore issues on critical information infrastructure protection and the law, including a preliminary analysis of the issue of information sharing between the public and private sectors. For more information, see <http://www.cstb.org/web/project_cip>.

[21]See, for example, Larry Ellison's October 8, 2001, article in the *Wall Street Journal*, "Digital IDs Can Help Prevent Terrorism," and Cara Garretson's December 2001 article in *CIO*, "Government Info Sharing Key to Fighting Terrorism," at <http://www.cio.com/government/edit/122001_share.html>.

[22]Loss of ID cards presents its own challenges to the system; if all of the individuals with lost IDs were to become immediately "suspect" in the system, intolerable backlogs and/or overload could result.

or detecting socially detrimental activities, because it avoids the uncertainty and confusion that may arise from multiple identities (notwithstanding that multiple identities can serve useful and socially desirable purposes, as described previously). Credit card companies, for example, can conduct behavior-pattern analysis for fraud detection.[23] Similar technologies must be used to detect behavior indicative of impending criminal or terrorist activities, although this raises concerns about profiling.

On the negative side, such analysis also enables invasions of personal privacy. The extent to which this occurs would depend heavily on the circumstances under which an individual can be compelled to present an ID, what information is retained, and which activities are tracked within the system (a topic explored above). Indeed, detecting a problem might only be possible in some instances through broad analysis. This would necessitate examining the behavior of many people who do not pose a risk—most human behavior involves law-abiding citizens pursuing constitutionally protected activities—in order to identify the few who do.[24]

---

[23]Credit card companies make these correlations using both standard statistical methods and neural networks.

[24]For a discussion of some of the effects and implications of ubiquitous surveillance cameras, see the October 7, 2001, article by Jeffrey Rosen, "A Watchful State," *New York Times Magazine*.

4

Concluding Remarks

Given the complexity of a nationwide identity system, its potential impacts, and the broad scope of the issues it raises, the committee believes that much more analysis is needed. Such analysis cannot proceed, however, without a clear articulation of the system's goals and requirements. The committee believes that if a nationwide identity system is to be created, the goals of such a system must be clearly and publicly identified and deliberated upon, with input sought from all stakeholders (including private citizens). Given the economic costs, the significant design and implementation challenges, and the risks to security and privacy posed by a poorly thought-out system, prior public review[1] is essential.

Thus the committee believes that proponents of a nationwide identity system should be required to present a very compelling case addressing these issues and that they should solicit input from a broad range of stakeholder communities.[2] The committee's own discussion of a nation-

---

[1]For an example of how this might work, consider the public-review cycle for the Advanced Encryption Standard (AES); see <http://csrc.nist.gov/encryption/aes/>, managed by the National Institute of Standards and Technology.

[2]Other stakeholder groups have already commented on the idea of a national identity card, albeit within varying contexts. For example, in 1995 the Cato Institute presented an extensive policy analysis of the notion of a nationwide worker registry within the context of a larger immigration debate (see <http://www.cato.org/pubs/pas/pa237.html>). The American Civil Liberties Union offered similar opposition (see <http://www.aclu.org/library/aaidcard.html>); around the same time, Privacy International prepared a report describing the use and implications of national ID cards from an international perspective (see <http://www.privacy.org/pi/activities/idcard/idcard_faq.html>).

wide identity system, although brief and modest in scope, raised numerous complex questions. It is clear that an evaluation of the potential costs, presumed benefits, and potential drawbacks of any proposed system is necessary in order to fully appreciate its trade-offs.

Care must be taken to completely explore the ramifications of any nationwide identity system not only because of the significant policy concerns and technological challenges but also because after-the-fact costs—the result of revoking, correcting, or redesigning after broad deployment—would be enormous. Moreover, analysts must give serious consideration to the idea that—given the broad range of potential uses, security requirements, and privacy needs that might be contemplated—no single nationwide identity system is likely to meet the varied demands of all potential users. Undoubtedly many more issues exist that are not even touched upon here.

Given the wide range of technological and logistical challenges, the likely direct and indirect costs, the serious potential for infringing on the rights and freedoms of ordinary citizens, and the gravity of the policy issues raised, any proposed nationwide identity system requires strict scrutiny and significant deliberation well in advance of design and deployment.

Appendixes

A

Committee Member and Staff Biographies

STEPHEN T. KENT, *Chair*, is chief scientist for information security at BBN Technologies, a division of Verizon Communications. During the last two decades, Dr. Kent's R&D activities have included the design and development of user authentication and access control systems, network layer encryption and access control systems, secure transport layer protocols, secure e-mail technology, multilevel secure (X.500) directory systems, and public-key certification authority systems. His most recent work focuses on security for Internet routing, very high-speed IP encryption, and high-assurance cryptographic modules. Dr. Kent served as a member of the Internet Architecture Board (1983-1994) and chaired the Privacy and Security Research Group of the Internet Research Task Force (1985-1998). He chaired the Privacy Enhanced Mail (PEM) working group of the Internet Engineering Task Force (IETF) from 1990 to 1995 and co-chairs the Public Key Infrastructure Working Group (1995-present). He is the primary author of the core IPsec standards: RFCs 2401, 2402, and 2406. He is a member of the editorial board of the *Journal of Computer Security* (1995-present), serves on the board of the Security Research Alliance, and served on the board of directors of the International Association for Cryptologic Research (1982-1989). Dr. Kent was a member of CSTB's Information Systems Trustworthiness Committee (1996-1998), which produced *Trust in Cyberspace*. His other previous NRC service includes the CSTB Committee on Rights and Responsibilities of Participants in Networked Communities (1993-1994), the Technical Assessment panel for the NIST Computer Systems Laboratory (1990-1992), and the CSTB Secure

Systems Study Committee (1988-1990). The U.S. Secretary of Commerce appointed Dr. Kent as chair of the Federal Advisory Committee to Develop a FIPS for Federal Key Management Infrastructure (1996-1998). The author of two book chapters and numerous technical papers on network security, Dr. Kent has served as a referee, panelist, and session chair for a number of conferences. Since 1977 he has lectured on the topic of network security on behalf of government agencies, universities, and private companies throughout the United States, Europe, Australia, and the Far East. Dr. Kent received the B.S. degree in mathematics summa cum laude from Loyola University of New Orleans and the S.M., E.E., and Ph.D. degrees in computer science from the Massachusetts Institute of Technology. He is a fellow of the Association for Computing Machinery and a member of the Internet Society and Sigma Xi.

MICHAEL ANGELO is currently a staff fellow at Compaq Computer Corporation and runs a laboratory at Compaq that assesses biometrics and other security-enhancing technologies, such as smart cards. He is considered a subject-matter expert for security and its associated technologies. His job is to provide technical guidance and input into strategic planning and the development of secure solutions. In addition, he is responsible for providing technical assistance to the corporate security team. Dr. Angelo possesses expertise in both biometric and token access authentication technology, including technical threat model and implementation analysis, as well as in risk reduction enhancement methodology, applied computer system security, computer forensics, advanced data protection methodologies, and practical encryption techniques. His experience comprises 15 years in designing, implementing, managing, and supporting secure intra- and Internets, including gateways, firewalls, and sentinels, plus 20 years working at the kernel level of numerous operating systems, including a wide variety of hardware platforms (from PCs to supercomputers) and software platforms (including several flavors of UNIX, MS-DOS/Windows/NT, and VMS). He holds several patents. Dr. Angelo has been active in a number of trade standards organizations: the Trusted Computing Platform Association (TCPA), Americans for Computer Privacy (ACP), the Bureau of Export Administration Technical Advisory Committee (BXA-TAC), the Information Security Exploratory Committee (ISEC), the Key Recovery Alliance (KRA), the Computer Systems Policy Project, the Cross-Industry Working Team Security Working Group, and the National Institute of Standards and Technology's Industry Key Escrow Working Group.

STEVEN BELLOVIN is a fellow at AT&T Research. Dr. Bellovin received a B.A. degree from Columbia University and an M.S. and Ph.D. in computer science from the University of North Carolina at Chapel Hill. While a graduate student, he helped create Netnews; for this, he and the other collaborators were awarded the 1995 USENIX Lifetime Achievement Award. At AT&T Laboratories, he does research in networks and security and why the two do not get along. Dr. Bellovin has embraced a number of public interest causes and weighed in (e.g., through his writings) on initiatives (e.g., in cryptography and law enforcement) that appear to threaten privacy. He is currently focusing on cryptographic protocols and network management. Bellovin is the coauthor of the recent book *Firewalls and Internet Security: Repelling the Wily Hacker*, and he is a member of the Internet Architecture Board. He was a member of the CSTB committee that produced *Trust in Cyberspace* (1999), and he is a member of the National Academy of Engineering.

BOB BLAKLEY is chief scientist for security and privacy at IBM Tivoli Software in Austin, Texas. Dr. Blakley was chief scientist for DASCOM, Inc., at the time of its acquisition by IBM and integration into Tivoli. Before joining DASCOM, Dr. Blakley was lead security architect for IBM, where he was employed for 9 years. In addition to his product design responsibilities, Dr. Blakley led the IBM Security Architecture Board and was the IBM representative to the Open Group Security Program Group. He also served for 2 years as the chair of the OSF DME/DCE security working group. He is the author of *CORBA Security: An Introduction to Safe Computing with Objects*, published by Addison-Wesley. Dr. Blakley was also the editor of the Open Group PKI working group's "Architecture for Public Key Infrastructure." He has been involved in cryptography and data security design work since 1979 and has authored or coauthored seven papers on cryptography, secret-sharing schemes, access control, and other aspects of computer security. He was designated "Distinguished Practitioner" by the 2001 Annual Computer Security and Applications Conference. He is currently the general editor of the OASIS Security Services Technical Committee's SAML specification effort. He holds eight patents on security-related technologies. Dr. Blakley cochaired the ACM New Security Paradigms Workshop in 1997 and 1998, and he served on the program committees for several industry and academic conferences, including the NSA/OMG Distributed Object Computing Workshop, IEEE Security and Privacy, and ISOC Network and Distributed Systems Security (NDSS). Dr. Blakley received an A.B. in classics from Princeton University and a master's degree and Ph.D. in computer and communications sciences from the University of Michigan.

DREW DEAN is a computer scientist at SRI International. He joined SRI full time in July 2001; prior to that he was a member of the research staff at Xerox PARC. Dr. Dean holds M.A. and Ph.D. degrees from Princeton University and a B.S. degree from Carnegie Mellon University, all in computer science. He pioneered the systematic study of Java security and more recently has worked across a wide range of areas in security, including cryptography, the theory of access control, and IP traceback. He has received a Best Student Paper award from the ACM Computer and Communications Security conference (1997), an Outstanding Paper award from the ACM Symposium on Operating System Principles (1997), and a Best Paper award from the Internet Society's Network and Distributed Systems Security Symposium (2001). Dr. Dean is a member of the editorial board of Springer-Verlag's *International Journal of Information Security*.

BARBARA FOX is currently senior architect, Digital Rights Management and Cryptography, at Microsoft Corporation. She is coauthor of a number of research papers in the application of public key infrastructures to payment systems and, most recently, the IETF/W3C XML Digital Signature standard. Ms. Fox also serves on the board of directors for the International Financial Cryptography Association.

STEPHEN H. HOLDEN is an assistant professor in the Department of Information Systems at the University of Maryland, Baltimore County (UMBC). Dr. Holden's research, publications, and teachings leverage his substantial federal government experience in government-wide policy in information technology management and electronic government. Other research interests include information policy, electronic authentication policies and practices, and strategic management processes. He recently left the Internal Revenue Service (IRS) as a senior executive after a 16-year career in the federal career service. While at the IRS he served as the program executive, Electronic Tax Administration (ETA) Modernization, reporting to the assistant commissioner. Before that position in ETA he served as the national director of Electronic Program Enhancements. During that time he led efforts to develop new ETA programs, policies, and e-government systems for the IRS, including the ETA partnership effort, electronic payments, electronic authentication, and the IRS e-file promotional campaign. He also served on the federal Public Key Infrastructure Steering Committee. Prior to going to the IRS, Dr. Holden worked for 10 years at the Office of Management and Budget (OMB), doing a variety of policy, management, and budget analysis work. Significant accomplishments at OMB included drafting and completing a revision to the information technology management section of Circular A-130 and overseeing the publication of the first "Information Resource Management Plan of the Federal Government." Dr. Holden's career as a federal civil servant began in 1983 as a Presidential Management Intern at the Naval Sea Systems Command. He holds a Ph.D. (public administration and public affairs) from Virginia Polytechnic and State University and an M.P.A in public administration and a B.A. in public management from the University of Maine.

DEIRDRE MULLIGAN is director of the new Samuelson Law, Technology and Public Policy Clinic at the University of California, Berkeley, School of Law (Boalt Hall). While attending Georgetown University Law Center, Mulligan worked on the American Civil Liberties Union's privacy and technology project, where she honed her interest in preserving and enhancing civil liberties and democratic values. After law school, she became a founding member of the Center for Democracy and Technology, a high-tech, civil liberties public interest organization based in Washington, D.C. For 6 years, Mulligan was staff counsel at the center. She has worked with federal lawmakers, governmental agencies, the judicial system, public interest organizations, and the high-tech business community, with the goal of enhancing individual privacy on the Internet, thwarting threats to free speech on the Internet, and limiting governmental access to private data. She has testified in several settings and contributed to technical standards development. Ms. Mulligan received her J.D., cum laude, from Georgetown University Law Center in 1994 and a B.A. in architecture and art history from Smith College in 1988.

JUDITH S. OLSON is the Richard W. Pew Chair in Human Computer Interaction at the University of Michigan. She is also a professor in the School of Information, the Business School, and the Department of Psychology. Her research interests include computer-supported cooperative work, human-computer interaction, the design of business information systems for organizational effectiveness, and cognitive psychology. Professor Olson's recent research focuses on the nature of group work and the design and evaluation of technology to support it. This field combines cognitive and social psychology with the design of information systems. She began her career at the University of Michigan in the Department of Psychology, served as a technical supervisor for human factors in systems engineering at Bell Laboratories in New Jersey, and returned to Michigan to the Business School and the then-new School of Information. She has over 60 publications in journals and books and has served on a number of national committees, including the National Research Council Committee on Human Factors and the Council of the Association for Computing Machinery. She has recently been appointed to the CHI Academy of ACM's Special Interest Group on Computer-Human Interaction. Dr. Olson earned a B.A. in mathematics and psychology from

Northwestern University in 1965 and a Ph.D. 4 years later in the same disciplines from the University of Michigan.

JOE PATO is currently the principal scientist for the trust, security, and privacy research program at HP Labs and has served as the CTO for Hewlett-Packard's Internet Security Solutions Division. Mr. Pato's current research focuses on the trust needs of collaborative enterprises on the Internet, addressing both interenterprise models and the needs of lightweight information appliances representing the interests of the individual. He is looking at critical infrastructure protection and the confluence of trust, e-services, and mobility. This work recently led him to be one of the founders of the Information Technology Information Sharing and Analysis Center (IT-ISAC). His past work has included the design of delegation protocols for secure distributed computation; key exchange protocols; interdomain trust structures; the development of public- and secret-key-based infrastructures; and the more general development of distributed enterprise environments. Mr. Pato is currently cochair of the OASIS Security Services Technical Committee and has participated on several IEEE, ANSI, and NIST standards or advisory committees.

RADIA PERLMAN is a Distinguished Engineer at Sun Microsystems Laboratories. She is the architect for a group that does research in network security issues, recently focused on PKI deployment. Some of the group's implementation will be distributed as part of a reference implementation for Java. She is the author of many papers in the field of network security, as well as coauthor of a textbook on network security and author of a textbook on lower-layer networking protocols. She is also well known for her work on sabotage-proof routing protocols. Her work on lower-layer protocols is also well known and forms the basis of modern bridging, switching, and routing protocols. This expertise is crucial to understanding the technology behind such things as providing Internet anonymity. She has about 50 issued patents, a Ph.D. in computer science from MIT, and S.B. and S.M. degrees in mathematics from that institution. She was recently awarded an honorary doctorate from KTH, the Royal Institute of Technology, Sweden.

PRISCILLA M. REGAN is an associate professor in the Department of Public and International Affairs at George Mason University. Prior to joining that faculty in 1989, she was a senior analyst in the Congressional Office of Technology Assessment (1984-1989) and an assistant professor of politics and government at the University of Puget Sound (1979-1984). Since the mid-1970s, Dr. Regan's primary research interest has been the analysis of the social, policy, and legal implications of organizational use of new information and communications technologies. Dr. Regan has published over 20 articles or book chapters, as well as *Legislating Privacy: Technology, Social Values, and Public Policy* (University of North Carolina Press, 1995). As a recognized researcher in this area, Dr. Regan has testified before Congress and participated in meetings held by the Department of Commerce, the Federal Trade Commission, the Social Security Administration, and the Census Bureau. Dr. Regan received her Ph.D. in government from Cornell University in 1981 and her B.A. from Mount Holyoke College in 1972.

JEFFREY I. SCHILLER received his S.B. in electrical engineering (1979) from the Massachusetts Institute of Technology. As MIT network manager he has managed the MIT Campus Computer Network since its inception in 1984. Prior to his work in the Network Group, he maintained MIT's Multics timesharing system during the time frame of the ARPANET TCP/IP conversion. He is an author of MIT's Kerberos Authentication system. Mr. Schiller is the Internet Engineering Steering Group's (IESG) area director for security. He is responsible for overseeing security-related working groups of the Internet Engineering Task Force (IETF). He was responsible for releasing a U.S. legal freeware version of the popular PGP encryption program. Mr. Schiller is also responsible for the development and deployment of an X.509-based PKI at MIT. He is the technical lead for the new Higher Education Certifying Authority being operated by the Corporation for Research and Educational Networking (CREN). Mr. Schiller is also a founding member of the Steering Group of the New England Academic and Research Network (NEARnet). NEARnet, now part of Genuity, Inc., is a major nationwide Internet service provider.

SOUMITRA SENGUPTA is assistant professor in the Department of Medical Informatics at Columbia University. Dr. Sengupta has focused his work on the challenges of security and privacy in health care, complementing his academic work by service as security officer for the New York-Presbyterian Healthcare System. His research interests are in the areas of distributed systems, their monitoring, management, and security aspects, and their application in a health care environment. He is interested in the architectural design and engineering concerns of building large, functioning systems over heterogeneous platforms and protocols. Dr. Sengupta holds a B.E. from Birla Institute of Technology and Science (electrical and electronics engineering), Pilani, India, and M.S. and Ph.D. degrees in computer science from the State University of New York at Stony Brook. He was a member of the Association for Computing Machinery (ACM) from 1984 to 1994 and the Institute for Electrical and Electronic

Engineers (Computer Society) from 1984 to1992, and is currently a member of the American Medical Informatics Association.

JAMES L. WAYMAN has been the director of the Biometrics Test Center at San Jose State University in San Jose, California, since 1995. The center is funded by the United States and other countries to develop standards and scientific test and analysis methods and to advise on the use or non-use of biometric identification technologies. The test center served as the U.S. National Biometrics Test Center from 1997 to 2000. Dr. Wayman received the Ph.D. degree in engineering from the University of California at Santa Barbara in 1980 and joined the faculty of the Department of Mathematics at the U.S. Naval Postgraduate School in 1981. In 1986, he became a full-time researcher for the Department of Defense in the areas of technical security and biometrics. Dr. Wayman holds three patents in speech processing and is the author of dozens of articles in books, technical journals, and conference proceedings on biometrics, speech compression, acoustics, and network control. He serves on the editorial boards of two journals and on several national and international biometrics standards committees. He is a senior member of the Institute of Electrical and Electronic Engineers.

DANIEL J. WEITZNER is director of the World Wide Web Consortium's Technology and Society activities. As such, he is responsible for development of technology standards that enable the Web to address social, legal, and public policy concerns such as privacy, free speech, protection of minors, authentication, intellectual property, and identification. He is also the W3C's chief liaison to public policy communities around the world and a member of the ICANN Protocol Supporting Organization's Protocol Council. Mr. Weitzner holds a research appointment at MIT's Laboratory for Computer Science and teaches Internet public policy at MIT. Before joining the W3C, Mr. Weitzner was cofounder and deputy director of the Center for Democracy and Technology, an Internet civil liberties organization in Washington, D.C. He was also deputy policy director of the Electronic Frontier Foundation. As a leading figure in the Internet public policy community, he was the first to advocate user control technologies such as content filtering and rating to protect children and avoid government censorship of the Internet. These arguments played a critical role in the 1997 U.S. Supreme Court case *Reno v. ACLU*, awarding the highest free speech protections to the Internet. He successfully advocated the adoption of amendments to the Electronic Communications Privacy Act, creating new privacy protections for online transactional information such as Web site access logs. Mr. Weitzner has a degree in law from Buffalo Law School and a B.A. in philosophy from Swarthmore College. His publications on communications policy have appeared in the *Yale Law Review*, *Global Networks*, *Computerworld*, *Wired*, *Social Research*, *Electronic Networking: Research, Applications & Policy*, and *Whole Earth*. He is also a commentator for NPR's Marketplace Radio.

STAFF

LYNETTE I. MILLETT is a study director and program officer with the Computer Science and Telecommunications Board of the National Research Council. She is currently involved in several CSTB projects along with the authentication study, including a comprehensive exploration of privacy in the information age and a study examining the fundamentals of computer science. She is also exploring possible study options for CSTB with respect to the issues of open source software development, dependability of complex software systems, and women in computer science. She recently completed the CSTB study that produced *Embedded, Everywhere: A Research Agenda for Networked Systems of Embedded Computers*. Before joining CSTB, she was involved in research on static analysis techniques for concurrent programming languages as well as research on value-sensitive design and informed consent online. She has an M.Sc. in computer science from Cornell University. Her undergraduate degree is in mathematics and computer science from Colby College. Her graduate work was supported by both an NSF graduate fellowship and an Intel graduate fellowship. While at Cornell, Ms. Millett cofounded its Engineering Graduate Student Association.

JENNIFER BISHOP is a senior project assistant with the Computer Science and Telecommunications Board of the National Research Council. Before moving to Washington, Ms. Bishop worked for the City of Ithaca, New York, coordinating the Police Department's transition to a new SQL-based time accrual and scheduling application. Her other work experience includes designing customized hospitality industry performance reports for Ithaca-based RealTime Hotel Reports, LLC, maintaining the police records database for the City of Ithaca, and hand-painting furniture for Mackenzie-Childs, Ltd., of Aurora, New York. She is an artist working in oil and mixed media and is currently attempting to make her professional debut on the Washington art scene. Ms. Bishop holds a B.F.A (2001) in studio art from Cornell University.

B

What Is CSTB?

As a part of the National Research Council, the Computer Science and Telecommunications Board (CSTB) was established in 1986 to provide independent advice to the federal government on technical and public policy issues relating to computing and communications. Composed of leaders from industry and academia, CSTB conducts studies of critical national issues and makes recommendations to government, industry, and academic researchers. CSTB also provides a neutral meeting ground for consideration of complex issues where resolution and action may be premature. It convenes invitational discussions that bring together principals from the public and private sectors, assuring consideration of all perspectives. The majority of CSTB's work is requested by federal agencies and Congress, consistent with its National Academies context.

A pioneer in framing and analyzing Internet policy issues, CSTB is unique in its comprehensive scope and effective, interdisciplinary appraisal of technical, economic, social, and policy issues. Beginning with early work in computer and communications security, cyberassurance and information systems trustworthiness have been a cross-cutting theme in CSTB's work. CSTB has produced several reports known as classics in the field, and it continues to address these topics as the fields grow in importance.

To do its work, CSTB draws on some of the best minds in the country, inviting experts to participate in its projects as a public service. Studies are conducted by balanced committees without direct financial interests in the topics they are addressing. Those committees meet, confer electronically, and build analyses through their deliberations. Additional expertise from around the country is tapped in a rigorous process of review and critique, further enhancing the quality of CSTB reports. By engaging groups of principals, CSTB gets the facts and insights critical to assessing key issues.

The mission of CSTB is to

- *Respond to requests* from the government, nonprofit organizations, and private industry for advice on computer and telecommunications issues and from the government for advice on computer and telecommunications systems planning, utilization, and modernization;
- *Monitor and promote the health of the fields* of computer science and telecommunications, with attention to issues of human resources, information infrastructure, and societal impacts;
- *Initiate and conduct studies* involving computer science, technology, and telecommunications as critical resources; and
- *Foster interaction* among the disciplines underlying computing and telecommunications technologies and other fields, at large and within the National Academies.

As of March 2002, CSTB activities with security and privacy components address privacy in the information age, critical information infrastructure protection, authentication technologies and their privacy implications, information technology for countering terrorism, and geospatial information systems. Additional studies examine broadband, digital government, the fundamentals of computer science, limiting children's access to pornography on the Internet, digital archiving and preservation, and Internet navigation and the domain name system. Explorations touching on security and privacy are under way in the areas of the insider threat, cybersecurity research, cybersecurity principles and practices, dependable/safe software systems, wireless communications and spectrum management, open source software, digital democracy, the "digital divide," manageable systems, information technology and journalism, supercomputing, and information technology and education.

For more information on CSTB, see its Web site at <http://www.cstb.org>; write to CSTB, National Research Council, 2101 Constitution Avenue, N.W., Room HA 560, Washington, DC 20418; call at (202) 334-2605; or e-mail the CSTB at cstb@nas.edu.